shut up from the kindness of are freely permitted to visit m. / Here too is a side wind he negro houses. It is rel- t of repair, and when a... ...ing to the m... ...head... hink i... ...injustice to be ...ee or fra...they h.ve n.

ofter sex say to this ? ...who are owners of slaves, ...without any scruple, order flogged; and some of them to see them stripped bare, e usual disgusting manner." f our peregrinations through er met with any of these vi- know of no body else, who t such exhibitions; and as

...can carry home... we... rich on the... cient to... ...arse... ...vour. ...e depth of... attenuated bo... picture; it ma... life in... ...natu... powerfu... British empi... bouring popu... to Ireland, w... pestilence re... and madness... been declare... cending rapi... no sorrows...

ROSE HALL

ROSE HALL

Jamaica

Story of a People...
a Legend...
and a Legacy

Published By Rose Hall Limited In Association with Kingston Publishers Limited

1

Prologue

From the time that my wife, Linda, and I first looked upon the Rose Hall Estate, with the ruins of the Great House rising like a colossus out of the foothills, we considered it an opportunity.

An opportunity to restore that legendary (wreck) Ruin to its former grandeur; an opportunity to share in the creation of a viable economy for the wonderful people of Montego Bay: an opportunity to make Jamaica a home for ourselves.

Now all of those things have come to pass. But the effort and cooperation required from the very many dedicated people is a continuing process.

Together with the Jamaicans, and especially the people of St. James Parish, we have forged new plans to make Rose Hall a paradise unequalled in the Caribbean.

The natural setting is well known—the fabulous azure sea; the clean, white beaches; the rich soil and lush growth; the foothills rising into lofty peaks provide those who ascend them a rare view of serene tranquility. Jamaica is truly a land of enchantment rich in people, legend and legacy.

For it is the people of Jamaica who are the country's greatest treasure. They are a friendly, proud and self-reliant people. It is with their collaboration that we brought into their community facilities to accommodate large conventions of visitors, and to restore not only the fabled Great House but also adjacent landmarks such as Mount Zion Church. They, it is, who have made possible the new housing for people who might never have afforded it otherwise, and most significantly, a growing prosperity creating skilled craftsmen with more and more opportunities to build a better Jamaica.

The Jamaicans have lived in harmony with their land since long before Columbus became the first European to set foot on the island. They overcame an interlude of slavery to establish a tradition of freedom and created an independent nation as meaningful and proud as that of any other country in the world. Their music and dance have spanned the continents, their folk

I

art has won the enduring admiration of many other peoples, and their products such as sugarcane, bauxite and mahogany are an intrinsic part of our world economy.

Each return to Jamaica brings new enchantment from the freshness of this remarkable country and the continued friendliness and cooperation of the people who, alone, have the resources and the capacity to make a nation great.

Jamaica is great. It is an entire culture encapsulated in a tiny part of the earth's land mass. And whether one goes there for a short visit or for a more permanent stay as we have, one will find that it more than meets the foremost challenge of life, which is to continually open new horizons.

It is our hope that this book will help the reader to find a way into Jamaica.

John W. Rollins

2

Jamaica–Land of People, Wood & Water

Some 1.8 million Jamaicans live on 4,411 square miles of mountainous island country which lies between the 17th and 18th parallels of latitude, and which is roughly 150 miles long by 50 miles wide. Lying some 90 miles off the south coast of Cuba, Jamaica enjoys a climate tempered by northeasterly trade winds which blow all the year round.

The soft, sibilant word, "Xaymaca" was the name the Arawaks gave to the Island and which the Spaniards translated into the phrase, "the land of wood and water". It still retains that characteristic, but has evolved since Christopher Columbus first landed in 1494 on the sand-fringed shores supporting rising peaks of forested terrain, into a land of people. The people are rich in their splendid diverse origins, presenting to civilization and the world a new people—vital, energetic, catalystic and decidedly complex. The sources of origin are largely from the old world since the aboriginal Arawaks died out with the advent of European diseases as much as with the demands for hard and strenuous labour, as chronicles claim. At the time that Martin Luther was creating dissension in Church circles in Germany, Africans were being introduced to the Island in 1517 from the west coast of Africa. They brought with them as well a variety of tribal customs that reached from what is now Mali to the far reaches of the River Congo.

They worked the sugar plantations under European overlords in a slave society that bred suspicion, demoralisation and fear. But it also bred among the majority of the people inner reserves of power, great resilience and a capacity for adapting and creating a new society in the face of great odds in their new environment.

Emancipation!

And all the resources of the invincibility of the human spirit were ploughed into the great task of rehabilitation and the creation of a free society. There was the help of Christian missionaries like Hope Waddell who supervised the building of Mount Zion Church which overlooks Rose Hall, and even of former masters. But most of all there was the will of the people to rehumanize themselves and build a just and civilized community of men and women.

But the continuing need for cheap labour brought still more people. This time the sources were the Orient—the Deccan Plateau of India, the Canton Valley of China, Europe, Africa, the Far East and still later the Near East with merchant immigrants arriving from Lebanon!

Intermarriage and miscegenation which started with the Europeans and Africans continued with the other ethnic groups, and the result has been a mosaic of people—all different but sharing in the common heritage of foreign people to create a new life on foreign soil.

The deepening of colonialism in the 1860's brought new challenges, and again the people struggled over the hurdles to produce a period of creative ferment and abiding hope.

The result was the saga of 1938 which marked the beginning of the self-government movement and a social revolution that propelled the majority of people into the political and civic wheels of the country. Now, nearly four decades later, many hopes for development and progress remain to be fulfilled, and the people continue their noble struggle for liberation and independence.

Contradictions abound in Jamaica so that complexity is commonplace. The sturdy independence of the peasant owning his few acres of hillside land, the assertive vigour of the urban hopeful in search for a better life, the aggressiveness of the striving middle and professional class, even the Jamaicaness of the scions of the old plantocracy and the urban mercantile group all reflect a seriousness of aim and purpose in this land of water, wood and people. But it sometimes hides a capacity for living and an incomparable sense of humour in people capable of laughing at themselves.

Sense of humour comes out mostly in the folkways and folkspeech of the people. "In the beginning was the 'WORD' "—and the 'WORD' indeed weighs heavily in the life-style of the Jamaican people—long, sonorous and spontaneous words. Scholars have derived the Jamaican dialect largely from European, English and West African language-patterns. Louise Bennett, the folk poet of Jamaica, has caught humour and music in priceless quatrains, and two scholars have recorded it in a well-researched dictionary. It is immortalized in the daily utterances of most of the people of Jamaica who introduce variations into the established themes at the drop of a hat, and thus produce a living treasure for the Island. It is the wry fables of Brer Anancy, who can outwit the strength of the lion, the size of the elephant and the cunning of the snake. It is the speech through which the people on plantations communicated and sang, and told their legends. Jamaica, a legendary landscape—Rose Hall, Three-Finger Jack, Lover's Leap!

Jamaica is rich in song and story. And ritual too! Here the heritage of Africa comes up strongest. It is preserved especially in a storehouse of religious ceremonies which can still be seen from St. Thomas, in the east, to the western end of the island in the Parish of Hanover. To the rhythm of drums, the people rock and sway in their wayside churches of their "Pocomania" gatherings.

St. James, the parish which houses Rose Hall Estate, was and still is the scene of Jamaican folk ritual and social dance, and much of this is preserved to this day among the people, as well as in formal presentations by dance and theatre groups, and through the annual festivals.

Africa is reincarnated too in the contemporary expressions of music in the Rastafarian moods and lifestyle, in the majority of Jamaicans' concern for that part of their heritage long denigrated though never totally subdued.

The people who sing and dance and tell their fables also work. Industries jostle with traditional agriculture to produce a variety of lifestyles ranging from the highly complex and sophisticated industrial enterprise, that is bauxite and alumina, (from which aluminum is made,) through the service 'industry' of tourism, to the growing of cane and the manufacture of sugar. For Jamaica is an agricultural country. It grows other crops as well—bananas, citrus, ginger, pimento and some coffee in the mountains.

Mountains! "All men come to the hills, finally," mused one of Jamaica's more distinguished writers. More than half the 4,411 square miles are hill country. This is the country that protected the runaway Maroon slaves under the Spanish occupation from 1509 to 1655, when the English finally came. And this same hill country it was that embraced the newly-freed slaves in 1838 when they acquired land away from the plantations in the plains and preserved their hard-won freedom. The hills are protective and strong. Standing back away from them one is forced to agree with Roger Mais, the writer, that the hills are indeed joyful together.

Another Jamaican writer, John Hearne, describes his country as "a long jagged backbone of mountains set in a ring of gently sloping plain which varies in depth, from a ribbon under sheer, forested walls on the north-east to wide, dry savannahs on the southwest. The Blue Mountains on the East are high, peaks of five to six thousand feet jumbled around the seven thousand four hundred foot of the Peak. It is a terrain of steep misty valleys funnelling up to the peaks, long ridges, narrow as a mule's spine, with cool, tart air blowing up the flanks under the rain-clouds.'

It is this kind of land that attracts loyalties. A thriving tourist economy with clients largely from North America but also from Europe bears testimony to this fact. But more so with the hundreds of thousands of Jamaicans who live abroad in America, Great Britain, Canada and parts of Latin America but who retain their Jamaican identity, visit their homeland periodically and harbour warm and firm sentiments about the land of their birth.

One great Jamaican leader in response to this, enthusiastically affirmed his countrymen to be a great people. 'Out of the past of fire and suffering and neglect,' he noted, 'the human spirit has survived—patient and strong, quick to anger, quick to forgive, lusty and vigorous, but with deep reserves of loyalty and love, and a deep capacity for steadiness under stress, and for the joy in all the things that make life good and blessed.'

The joy is in the people who, hard-headed and practical, are surely all blessed. The joy is in their land with its legend and its beauty...and the joy is in their legacy with its hope and promise for tomorrow. ✿

Political and Cultural Development

The culture of Jamaica is as rich and complex as the social matrix, as diffuse as the landscape, as diverse as the faces of Jamaicans. It is the culture of a new nation in the process of defining itself, a reflection of political Independence achieved in 1962. In the search for self-expression, more than 300 years of cross-cultural influences are readily apparent, but much is transformed and illuminated by a consciousness that is uniquely Jamaican. How else, for instance, can one explain the country buses called "Ali Baba," "The Lone Ranger" or "Hamlet, Prince of Denmark," or the handcartman cadging a living selling coconuts who has neatly lettered on one side of his cart "Hollywood Star," and on the other side the bold assertion that "In God We Trust."

In Jamaica there is a culture that is part of an international mainstream — Shakespeare or Genet performed by one of the half dozen or so semi-professional theatrical companies; the "uptowners" in evening clothes off to the theatre to hear the famous visiting violinist; there are ballet lessons and art schools. There are Jamaican artists whose paintings are hung in international museums, and writers and musicians who have received critical acclaim in the wider world. Pervading all is the best of the local Reggae music, the same beat which issues from wayside bars, that is heard in the distortion of the transistor radio which to many Jamaicans is the foremost extension of himself.

There are foot-stomping religious revivals in the hills, Harvest Festivals and lively wakes for the dead, the survival of African rituals, the drumming of Rastafari and the exuberance of religious cultists who worship with chants and rituals. There are dialect verses and Anancy folk tales and digging songs and birth customs which survive from our earlier, oral tradition. Bridging the gap between the modern and the traditional, the sophisticated and the primitive, the African and the Western, are groups like the National Dance Theatre Company and the Jamaican Folk Singers who have won critical acclaim overseas and steadfast loyalty at home for their fusion of sophisticated techniques with the Jamaican folk idiom.

Jamaica today is in the throes of what many regard as a cultural revolution and like other countries at a similar stage of development, the significant question is: What is a Jamaican culture? The question would hardly have arisen a few generations ago, because the Jamaican ethos until recently reflected little more or less than a pale imitation of the British way of life. What is being born today is a culture rooted in diverse origins but insistently reflecting the Jamaican way of life. In order to understand the vitality in Jamaican art, music and performing arts today, one must understand the centuries that went before, in which any form of native or original expression, was stultified, and in the case of the African slaves — the progenitors of the vast majority of

Jamaicans today — deliberately suppressed. It is therefore not accidental that the cultural revolution has been given new impetus by the widening of political participation and the fact of political Independence. In fact, the earliest development of a Jamaican culture is inextricably tied to the rise of nationalism and to the "social revolution" which began with the political ferment of some thirty years ago. Thus many Jamaicans living today have lived through virtually the entire time-span marking the development of indigenous culture. Happily, in the process of discovering themselves, Jamaicans are also finding that fragments of the African legacy, especially in music, have lain dormant over the centuries, waiting to be rediscovered by a new generation.

In seeking to discover a Jamaican culture we must also understand that all Jamaicans reflect transplants from other cultures whether British, African, Chinese, Jewish, Arabic or Indian at different times in history. This presents both the difficulty of deciding where the current cultural emphasis should lie, as well as the exciting promise of fusing out of disparate elements a culture that in the world could well become unique.

Nothing remains of the original inhabitants of Jamaica, the Arawak Indians, who died out within a few decades of the discovery of the Island by Christopher Columbus in 1494. Little also remains of the Spanish rule which ended in 1655 when the Island was captured by the British. As a primary sugar producer, Jamaica in the seventeenth century soon became one of the most valuable colonies in the vast British holdings throughout the world. Up to 1883, the trinity of slavery, the plantation system and colonial rule dictated a society described as "materialistic and brutal" with little desire or outlet for cultural development. Emancipation in 1838 created a free peasantry, but after the brutalisation of slavery, little remained evident of the rich cultures the ex-slaves had left behind in their homelands. As a people cut off at the roots, they had few avenues of self-expression or little consciousness of their cultural potential outside of the European model of their former masters. The educational pattern catered to an elite of "free men of colour" and patterned as it was on the English model, merely served to reinforce the acquisition of European habits and customs. In an essay on "Our Heritage" Jamaican writers Hearne and Nettleford point out the all-pervasive nature of cultural imitation: *"the fact that this imitation was servile, sometimes clumsy and often ridiculous should not blind us to the fact that it was also thorough. It might have been uncreative and in some ways stifling, but it deeply penetrated into the consciousness of not only the brown middle class but also the black peasantry and working class."*

A system of government which for 300 years also denied the majority any political participation also mitigated against indigenous cultural development. Civil government in

Jamaica dates from 1661 and initially consisted of a Governor with an Advisory Council of 12 persons appointed by him and an elected Assembly consisting of English colonists. There were several constitutional changes over the years, the most significant taking place in 1830 when the franchise was extended to include free men of colour. Government nevertheless remained oligarchic, composed largely of wealthy planters and merchants. The Assembly form of government continued up to the 1860's when the grievances of the majority—the free peasantry excluded from decision-making—exploded in the 1865 "Morant Bay Rebellion." The Governor of the day reacted with extreme severity against the rioters and, in the ensuing outcry, the Assembly ceded its powers to the crown, and Jamaica became a crown colony. This new system of pure colonial rule threw into even sharper focus the problems of colonial people everywhere —the difficulty of attaining any self-definition beyond the imitation of colonial rulers.

The first major challenge to the total pervasiveness of European influences came in the 1920's when a black Jamaican named Marcus Garvey started the "Back to Africa" movement which gained with currency among Jamaicans and black people elsewhere, setting into motion for the first time thoughts about black culture and black consciousness.

At the same time, a black proletariat was in the process of evolving,

and new charismatic Jamaican leaders were waiting in the wings. The year 1938 is regarded as a watershed in Jamaican history, marking as it does, the division between the old and modern Jamaica. In that year, a colourful labour leader named Alexander Bustamante spearheaded islandwide agitation for better wages and working conditions for the masses. The "troubles" of '38 soon evolved into the demand by Jamaicans for increased participation in the running of their own affairs as Bustamante was joined by his cousin, Norman Manley, an eminent lawyer. Popular agitation eventually led to the granting of a New Constitution based on universal adult suffrage, and Jamaica's first election under the new franchise was held in 1944. Manley had already formed his People's National Party and Bustamante soon followed with the Jamaica Labour Party. In the first elections, the JLP emerged victorious but in succeeding elections, government has alternated between the two parties giving Jamaica a relatively stable two-party system of government. In 1957, further adjustments in the constitution were made to extend local political responsibility. The Executive Council established in 1944 was renamed the Cabinet, and the chairman became the Chief Minister. The British Governor was also removed from the Cabinet. In the late 1950's, Jamaica joined the Federation of the West Indies, but two years later opted out of the Federation to "go it alone" into Independence. On

August 6, 1962 the black, green and gold Jamaican flag flew for the first time, and Jamaica proudly took its place in the world of independent nations.

While retaining membership in the British Commonwealth and acknowledging the Queen of England as titular ruler, Jamaica now exercises complete control over her own affairs.

The titular Head of State is a native Governor-General acting as the Queen's Representative. The Prime Minister however, as leader of the majority party in the House of Representatives, is political Head of State. Jamaica's Parliament consists of an Upper and Lower House —the House of Representatives consisting of 53 elected members from which the inner council [the Cabinet] is drawn—and the Senate consisting of nominated members from both parties. Under the constitution, elections are held every five years. In March 1972, Jamaicans went to the polls for the eighth time and voted out of office the Jamaica Labour Party which had formed the government since Independence, bringing the opposition PNP into power with a large majority. The fact that change from ruling party to opposition was achieved by ballots rather than bullets is of tremendous international significance since Jamaica is one of the few newly-emergent nations to change the post-Independent government by peaceful means. Despite the ever-rising clamour for change in an Independent Jamaica, 300 years of British judicial and constitutional traditions have created a conservative streak which expresses itself most fully in the respect for the institutions of justice and parliamentary democracy. The new government has stated its intention of introducing significant changes to modernize Jamaica's legal and administrative machinery and increased attention to the country's social, cultural and economic development.

The growing nationalism of the thirties had launched the first art movement in Jamaica. In the social and political ferment of the times, Jamaican writers and artists along with the politicians began to question the values of the existing society while recognizing their native land as a source of inspiration. Thus for the first time artistic work was produced which mirrored the Jamaican experience. It meant for the first time the beginning of a Jamaican literature with themes and language reflecting the Jamaican society. Jamaican artists—largely untutored in these early days—began to engage in painting and sculpture; and the Jamaicanization of the school curriculum, to include studies in West Indian history and literature, accelerated the process towards the creation of a recognizable Jamaican culture.

The thinking which has evolved over the years is that Jamaicans must search for and develop all aspects of their cultural heritage and not just the European which has long prevailed. Since the vast majority of Jamaicans are of African origin there has also in recent years been a resurgence of interest in African culture given fresh impetus by the rise of African nationalism. The new Jamaican concern is also that the cultural bias should not only reflect the origins of the majority of the people but that all Jamaicans should be given the opportunity to participate in cultural and artistic development. Thus a great deal of recent cultural activity such as the National Festival and research into folk music and history have been government-inspired.

Political Independence has undoubtedly brought into serious questioning some of the underpinnings of the Jamaican social structure and an increasingly vocal demand for a redefinition of the values and orientation of the newly-emergent nation including cultural values.

The psychological freedom engendered by Independence unleashed a new wave of creativity in Jamaicans of all walks of life.

Poverty has proven no barrier to certain forms of cultural expression as can be seen in the development of pop music, one of the most significant achievements over the last decade and the birth of new dance forms and musical sounds gaining international currency—the Ska and Reggae which originally grew out of the music of the slums. The Rastafarians, a religious cult group, have also had significant impact on the wider Jamaican society in their music, their dress and in their increasing ventures into the fine arts, where many "primitive" painters are gaining attention and recognition.

The formation of the National Dance Theatre Company in 1962 not only gave Jamaica a disciplined dance company but also provided the stimulus and the instructors for a resurgence of dance as an art form throughout Jamaica. Straight theatrical groups have also become increasingly active giving to Jamaican audiences a wide selection in theatre ranging from the classical, foreign commercial hits to locally-written satirical reviews. An active Little Theatre Movement has staged a popular Christmas pantomime musical for over 21 years, and singing groups of a high standard have generated a resurgence of interest in folk music. Jamaican writers, historians and political scientists have also been engaged in the process of self-discovery and self-examination.

The single most important contributor to cultural development has been the annual Festival timed to coincide with the Independence celebrations in August. Festival includes everything from culinary arts to beauty contests. Festival has encouraged participation by thousands of Jamaicans of all ages in the hundreds of categories of competition available and has given rural Jamaicans especially, a chance to display and improve upon their skills whether at embroidery or poetry writing. Partly as a result of Festival, partly as a result of increased recognition of the need for the teaching of crafts and arts in schools, young Jamaican school children are being provided with new opportunities to develop their talents. In the cultural revolution, business interests have also begun to show tangible interest in artistic development. Rose Hall Developments, Ltd. is especially proud of its personal involvement in this direction through the creation of an annual art competition among the children of nearby Mount Zion Primary School.

Business firms on the whole have been encouraged to contribute to all forms of artistic enterprise from donating cash awards to Festival prize winners, to co-sponsorship of theatrical and dance performances to the commissioning of the works of Jamaican artists. The tourist industry has also become involved in helping those talented Jamaicans who cater largely to the tourist trade to develop and polish their skills. Under the auspices of the Jamaica Tourist Board for instance, night club performers are being given assistance by professionals; woodcarvers and artists whose works are geared primarily to the tourist market are also being given similar assistance.

Time was when any serious Jamaican artist — whether writer, painter or dancer—felt that he had to choose exile in one of the metropolitan countries because of his inability to survive in the Jamaican situation. In providing increased outlets for talented Jamaicans, the modern society is helping to minimize many of these frustrations, and the fact that talented Jamaicans are choosing to remain in their homeland and Jamaicans in exile are choosing to return, is an indicator of the development of a climate in which cultural endeavours can thrive and develop.

In the process, the creative arts as a self-conscious expression of the human spirit are developing side by side with the rediscovery of folk art and folk forms. In many areas the two are becoming fused in the new celebration of creativity and joy among the Jamaican people poised on the brink of self-discovery.✿

The Dream of Restoration

What started as a dream became a plan and the realisation of this plan stands ten minutes east of Montego Bay.—the internationally-famous tourist resort, surrounded by some 5,200 acres of sloping hills that sweep up into the mountains overlooking the Caribbean Sea. The boundaries date back two centuries and more; and its lands, long used for growing sugarcane, are as interesting historically as they are agriculturally. Once a thriving, profitable plantation, Rose Hall fell into ruin when Annee Palmer (the mistress of legendary proportions) was murdered in 1831.

It had to await the interest and enthusiasm of John Rollins, the American businessman and philanthropist to transform that part of the legend into reality...

The dream was always intended to offer greater economic, cultural and educational opportunities for Jamaicans as well as to offer added dimensions to the life of visitors to Jamaica...

Meticulous planning and cooperative spirit not only incorporated a restored Great House, but remained sensitive to the importance of maintaining the delicate equilibrium between man and his environment.

But it was in the restoration of the Great House that people realised the magic of discovery. Let Tom Concannon, chief architect in the restoration exercise speak for himself...

"My first acquaintance with Rose Hall Great House was early in 1961. What at that time was a gaunt, forlorn, rotting pile of masonry and timber fascinated me, and I was determined to do my utmost to see the mansion restored to its 18th-Century splendor. But how to do it? Where was the money to come from? I did not know, but set about finding out, after the National Trust Commission had formally 'listed' the ruin as a national monument on account of its architectural merit (which was apparent despite the ruined fabric) and its historic interest.

Unfortunately the combined efforts of various official sources to finance restoration work failed to find what was needed, thus leaving Rose Hall to continue its sad decline into a shabby and dangerous structure, the haunt of bats, owls, and—who knows?—spirits from the past. What little was left of the roof timbers fell to the ground, window openings became gaping gashes in the walls, giving the building an eerie, deserted, ghost-like appearance in keeping with its sinister reputation as the home of Annie Palmer, the legendary mistress of bygone days.

Toward the end of 1965, the restoration work I had done for the National Trust at Port Henderson led to my meeting with Mr. John W. Rollins and to his inviting me to do the work.

I had to commence in earnest to collate data I had already acquired and to search for answers to many puzzling features of the ruin that had baffled me. What, for example, had been the original appearance of the main north facade? Was the timber roof existing over the north deck, as indicated by metal ties and marks on the stonework, part of the early structure? These and many more questions had to be answered if we were to produce an authentic restoration.

Details of doors, windows, cornices and other features of a Georgian period house would not, of course, have been difficult to reproduce. Suddenly, I found a magic key! I was working in the West India Reference Library at the Institute of Jamaica in Kingston, when the Director, Bernard Lewis, located a file of photographs of Rose Hall taken about the turn of this century.

Of particular use was an excellent picture of the famed staircase, which according to local belief was removed by a former owner to be built into his Braemer house in Kingston some years ago. Another fortunate happening led to our greatest 'magic find' of all! Mr. James Henderson, the former owner, presented me with what I at once recognized as one of the actual carved fret designs from the renowned Rose Hall staircase, which had been taken from the Great House but not used in his Braemer house. This one piece gave us the exact tread and riser, the precise detail of scroll, and position of balusters to confirm what we had already gleaned from the old photographs."

After this it was further discoveries—and more magic. A search of the Kingston house basement produced an architectural gold mine comprising hundreds of carved and moulded fragments which had been removed from Rose Hall.

The result was an architectural jig-saw puzzle at first. But soon the problems were solved—a difficult but rewarding task. Tom Concannon describes the venture as a "truly fascinating and absorbing project which has already become an outstanding historical attraction for people from all parts of the world."

The restoration costing some one and a half million Jamaican dollars involved a new roof, new upper floor walls on the north and south elevations, rebuilding of the northwest corner of the north wall, new structural timbers and flooring, doors and windows throughout, and interior furnishings, which under the supervision of Mrs. John Rollins, reflect the care and research into authentic 18th-Century colonial styles.

And so the Rose Hall Great House, a national trust and monument, has been restored to its 18th-Century magnificence open to all the Jamaican people and their visitors for whom the monument must indeed have meanings deep and diverse. ✿

Land of Great Houses

Before the true history and the true legend be told of Rose Hall, it might fascinate the reader to know some more of the phenomenon of great houses in the plantation period of Jamaican history. These came at the end of an earlier era when the Island's wealth was procured from the sea's sweepings and freebooters' spoils. One can actually date it from the history-making earthquake of June 7, 1692 which sent the capital city of Port Royal below the sea. The Island indeed looked inward for growth and prosperity. The Island, it is said, settled down and the people built. The people built houses— "dwelling houses, counting houses, courthouses, sugarhouses and great houses."

For many generations sugarhouses received the greater attention from the commercial-minded plantocracy. As late as the 1770's a Jamaican historian, Edward Long, was writing that:

"It is but of late that the planters have paid much attention to elegance in their habitations ... it was not unusual to see a plantation adorned with a very expensive set of works, of brick or stone, well executed; and the owner residing in a miserable, thatched hovel, hastily put together with wattles and plaister, damp, unwholesome, and infested with every species of vermin. ...But the houses in general, as well in the country parts as in the towns, have been greatly improved within these last twenty years."

Rose Hall Great House was built within those "last twenty years,"

according to tradition. No longer could it be said as Charles Leslie did in 1739 that "one is not to look for the beauties of architecture here...." In a generation or two, Jamaica was to see fine examples of exquisitely-styled and well-furnished great houses in most parishes of the Island, furnishing the country with what a modern historian insists were "excellent examples of local building standards and evidence of a creole style, a Jamaican 'vernacular'...."

Tom Concannon agrees. For "from beginnings inspired by the Georgian period in England, architecture in Jamaica developed in a distinct manner of its own, based on classic forms and elements."

Two main styles were followed, the most common being a simple rectangular block; the other was a central block with wings. Cardiff Hall which stands some miles up the coast from Rose Hall is a good example of this. Others are Annandale near Lydford in St. Ann and the main house at Minard close to Brown's Town, also in the parish of St. Ann. Marlborough placed some 2000 feet in the hills of Manchester parish, is a good example of the second type. So is the Rose Hall Great House—easily one of the most impressive of its kind in the country. Near to Rose Hall is Cinnamon Hill another great house of repute, the past home of the Barretts and the Moultons who were the forebears of the poetess wife of Robert Browning. Today, a visit to Cinnamon Hill forms part of the "plantation tour" of the Rose Hall estates. Not far

away east of Cinnamon Hill lies Orange Valley Great House, a square block on three floors. And within half an hour's drive is Good Hope with its handsome 18th-Century great house, coach house, counting house, sugar works and estate hospital. Its Georgian character is distinctive. There are others as well— Brimmer Hall in St. Mary, Colbeck Castle in St. Catherine, Stokes Hall in St. Thomas, and Stewart Castle in Trelawny. They are in the care and trust of the people of Jamaica through the National Trust Commission.

What was life like in the great houses during the days when sugar was king? The general physical setting prepared the reader adequately.

Philip Gosse, a 19th-Century 'sojourner' in Jamaica had this to say: *"A flight of stone steps, with iron balustrades, on which run beautiful twining or creeping plants ... leads the visitor up to the front door, and he is immediately ushered into a spacious hall, of the form of a cross, extending the whole length and breadth of the house. This large hall is characteristic of all Jamaican houses; it forms the principal sitting room; and, from its shape, admits the cooling breeze to sweep through it, whenever there is a breath of air. The two square areas formed by one side of the cross are filled by bedrooms; but with these exceptions the whole of the sides and ends of the hall are either occupied by windows, or open, and furnished with jalousies, a broad sort of transverse venetian blinds,* which freely admit the air while they exclude the glare of light. . . . This large and cool apartment is furnished with sofas, ottomans, tables, chairs, etc., not differing from ours; but there is no fire place, nor any carpet. Instead of the latter the floor is made of the most beautiful of native woods, in the selection of which much taste is displayed, as also in the arrangement, so that the various colours of the wood may harmonise or contrast well with each other. Mahogany, greenheart, bread-nut, and blood-heart are among the trees whose timber is employed for floors. Great hardness is an indispensable requisite in the wood used, and capability of receiving a high polish, which is given and maintained with great labour. Scarcely anything surprises a European more than to tread on floors as beautifully polished as the finest tables of our drawing rooms. . . ."

The picture is one set for gracious living. But we are reminded that cooking was generally done in a kitchen detached from the main block via a covered way, such as at Rose Hall. Sanitary arrangements were primitive, and it was wise to be on the alert to avoid possible damage from waste thrown out of upper windows!

In the days of prosperity, 'when sugar was king,' life was enjoyed to the full. Eating and drinking were important items on the planter's agenda for the day, with an abundance of punch, ale and wine with the food. Sir Hans Sloane commented in 1667 on his work as a physician:

"The patients I had to do with, happened for the most part to have been jolly companions and drinkers," and mentioned a drinking bout where vast quantities were consumed before and at supper, concluding with the not unexpected observation:

"Both these gentlemen died since in England." The "general plenty and the magnificence of the tables" is mentioned by the historian Bryan Edwards at a later period.

With the decline in the fortunes of sugar, and the loss or reduction of cheap labour, economic conditions deteriorated in the 19th Century, bringing to an end the pattern of life in the balmy days of an earlier, more carefree period of prosperity.

With the disappearance of many of the great houses, Rose Hall therefore takes on new significance in the historical record of the Island's colourful past. ✿

Rose Hall–The Greatest Great House

But what is the true history of Rose Hall?

Joseph Shore's *In Old Saint James* gives a plausible account which tallies with material to be found in the Institute of Jamaica's West India Reference Library located in Kingston, the Island's capital.

Rose Hall's story begins with the purchase of a plantation, "True Friendship," near Montego Bay in the Parish of St. James, by Henry Fanning, in 1746. He secured 290 acres of rolling sugarcane land, bounded by the sea. Six months later, he married a parson's daughter, Rosa Kelly. She was a lovely woman, warm, cheerful and hospitable. Unfortunately, Fanning died six months after the marriage. In 1750, the widowed Rosa married a planter named George Ash. Although many records attribute the building of the famous Great House to Ash, the home he had built for his bride was actually a forerunner of the historic Great House.

Ash died in 1752, leaving poor Rosa very wealthy and a widow once more. She married her third husband the following year (1753), the Honourable Norwood Witter. He was most eligible and gallant when he courted Rosa, but he turned out to be an avaricious husband. He took liberally of her purse for the thirteen years of their marriage and died in 1766. The lovely lady had no lack of suitors and married for the fourth time in 1767. The Honourable John Palmer, Custos of St. James and a widower with two sons in England, became Rosa's

husband and the master of Rose Hall, along with the neighbouring estate of Palmyra, which he owned, it was he who built the Rose Hall Great House, recently restored, between 1770 and 1780.

The Great House was the finest residence in Jamaica. It had long, wide balconies; broad hewn stone steps led to an elegant portico on the main floor that opened onto a series of reception rooms. Magnificent carved mahogany staircases led from one floor to another, to the bedrooms, guest rooms, music room, dining rooms and salons. Throughout were thick mahogany doors, high ornamented arches, windows bedded in deep mahogany sills. The furnishings were just as exquisite.

According to Concannon, "..... *the main house was a rectangular stone and timber-framed structure rising three stories above ground and two stories on the south. It measured some 95 feet by 60 feet with a central portion on the north projecting 40 feet by 12 feet. The lower ground floor contained six rooms, probably used in part as staff and store rooms and perhaps as rest rooms for passing travellers, with doors to the gardens on the east and west and an internal staircase to the main ground floor.*

"*External and internal walls of the lower ground floor contained vertical slits, designed perhaps both for ventilation and as defence loopholes in time of attack. The ground or principal floor, the reception part of the mansion, had three rooms of great size, including a salon 40 feet*

by 25 feet placed axially along the north front, opening from a staircase hall 40 feet by 15 feet to the south, and a drawing room about 32 feet by 20 feet entered from these rooms on the east. There were two smaller rooms on the west, one perhaps the dining room for family occasions.

"*The upper floors contained five bedrooms, approached by a superb staircase in mahogany and other fine Jamaican timbers, rising across the west end of the stairs.*

"*Massive double doors in mahogany set axially on the northern facade led from the main salon to an open terrace running along the entire north elevation. The terrace was connected by a double flight of stone steps with the driveway on the north, leading to the lower canefields and the coast. The grounds were extensive with trees of many kinds and a flower garden to the east and south.*

"*Two covered arcades south of the main house swung to connect with single storied pavillions or wings that included, on the east, a music room and private quarters, and on the west a kitchen and stores, with servants' rooms at ground and lower ground floors.*

"*At each end of a terrace of the main house short flights of stone steps led to gardens at the lower level on east and west. This fine mansion was finished in a classical manner; there was timber panelling to doors and windows, a dado and cornice in the more important apartments, and rich joinery to semi-cir-*

cular headed double doorways onto the terrace and into the stairway hall.

"It is likely that some of the stone work came from England, shipped out as ballast; individual blocks for the north stairway were numbered in England for ease in building, and mason's marks can still be detected on stones of the main entrance.

"It was not uncommon to find on the indentured estate staff expert masons and carpenters, able to do first-class work; enough remains to testify excellent brick and stone craftsmanship, and it is known that joinery was of an equally high standard."

Magnificent Rose Hall was the most brilliant setting for assemblies of Jamaican society during the period when John and Rosa Palmer lived there. Their happy life together lasted twenty three years. Rosa died in 1790 having left all her property to John Palmer in a will written in 1777.

John Palmer married his third wife in 1792, a girl of twenty named Rebecca Ann James. He died just five years later leaving Rose Hall and Palmyra in trust for his two sons, John and James, their survivors and heirs and failing such heirs, to the sons of his nephew James Palmer. The young widow, Rebecca Ann Palmer, left Jamaica for England soon after her husband's death.

John and James Palmer, the sons of the first marriage, were absentee landlords and died in England without ever having visited Jamaica. Neither had children. Rose Hall and Palmyra thus reverted to the Honourable John Palmer's grand nephew, John Rose Palmer. He quickly set about possessing and taking care of his properties which had been carelessly handled for about twenty years.

In 1820, John Palmer married Annee May Patterson. This is the Annee Palmer who became the legend of Rose Hall. 🌹

For information on the following illustrations see Index of Illustrations on page XXVII

6

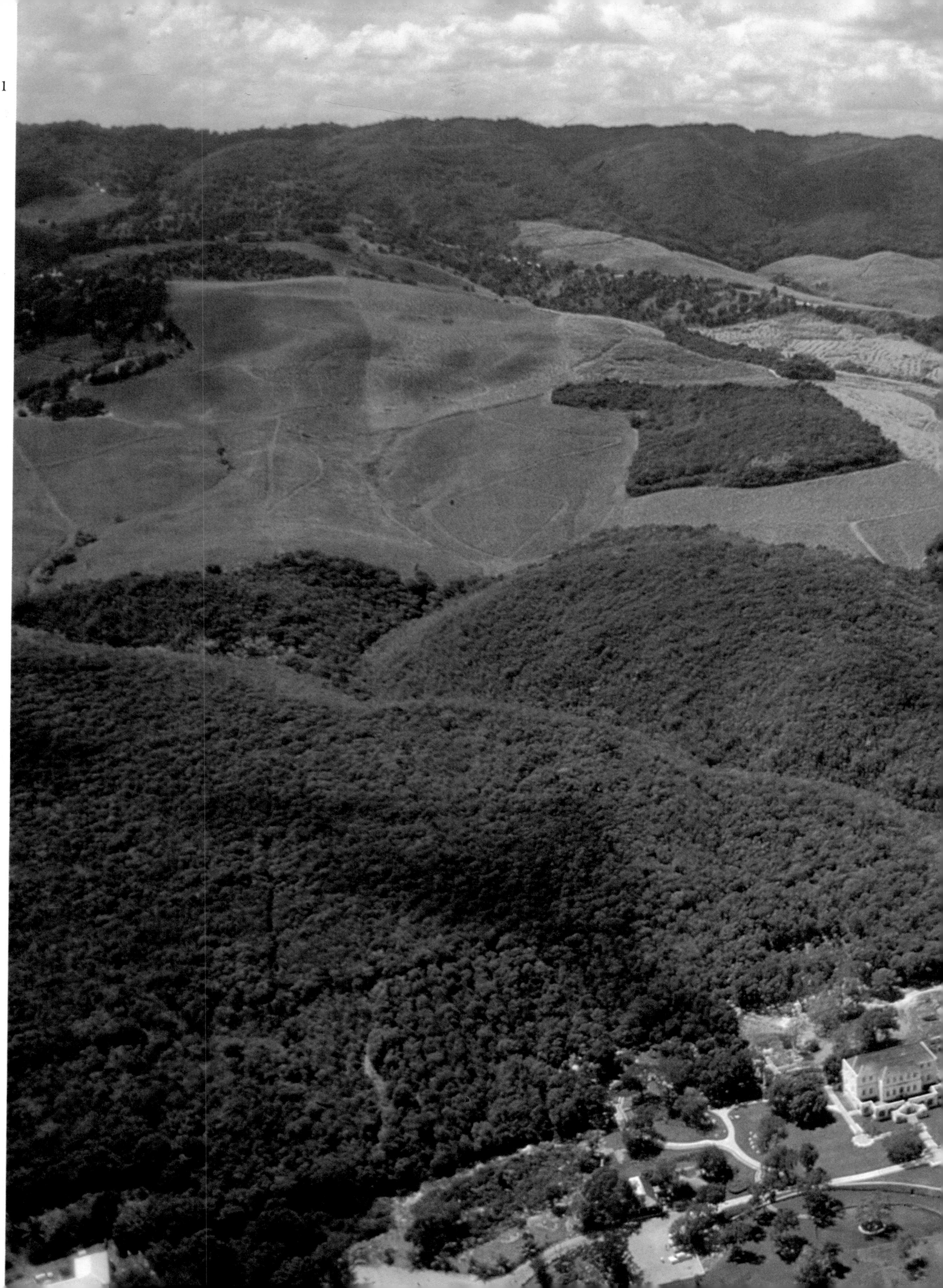

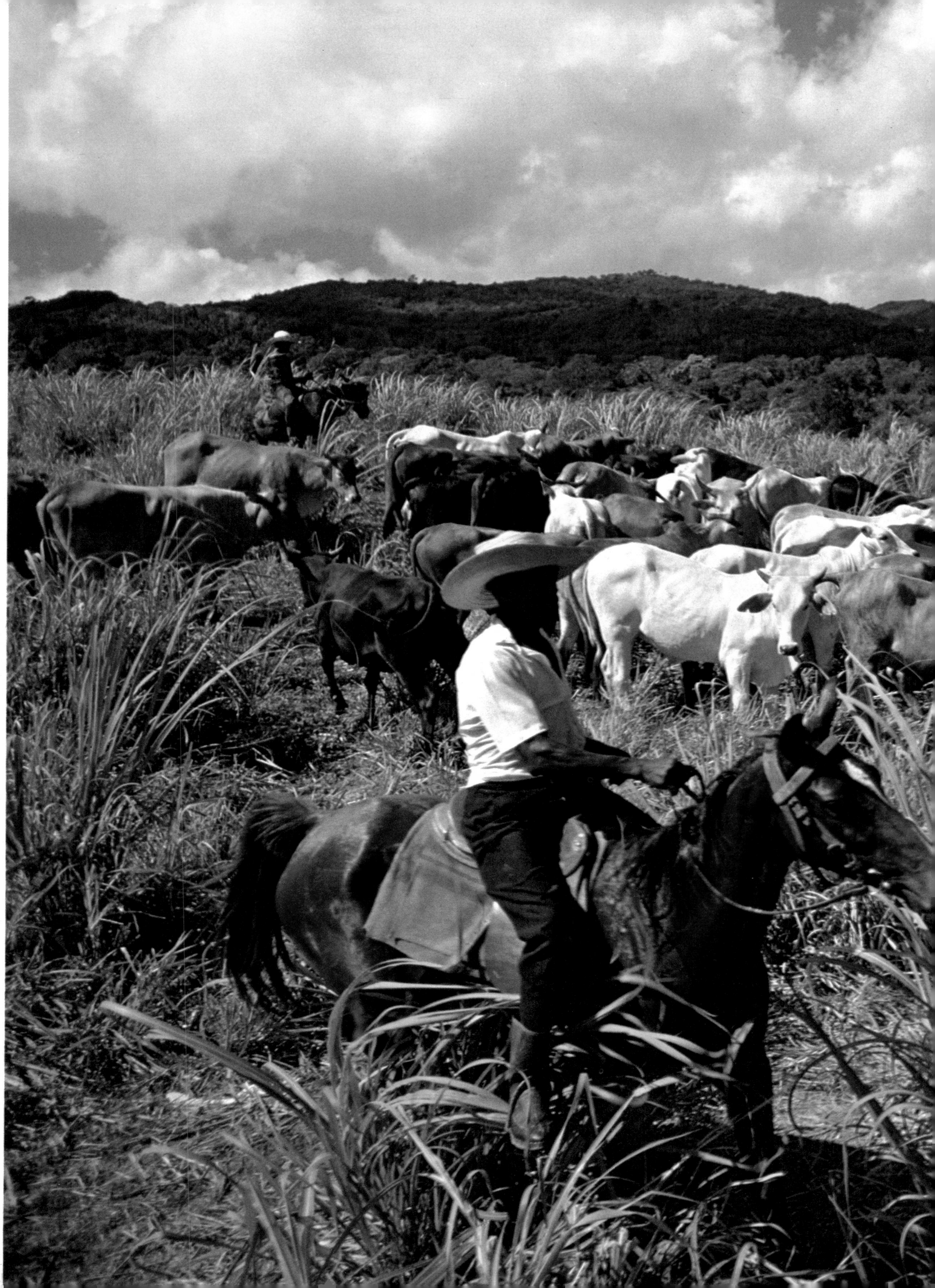

15

ROSE HALL EXPER

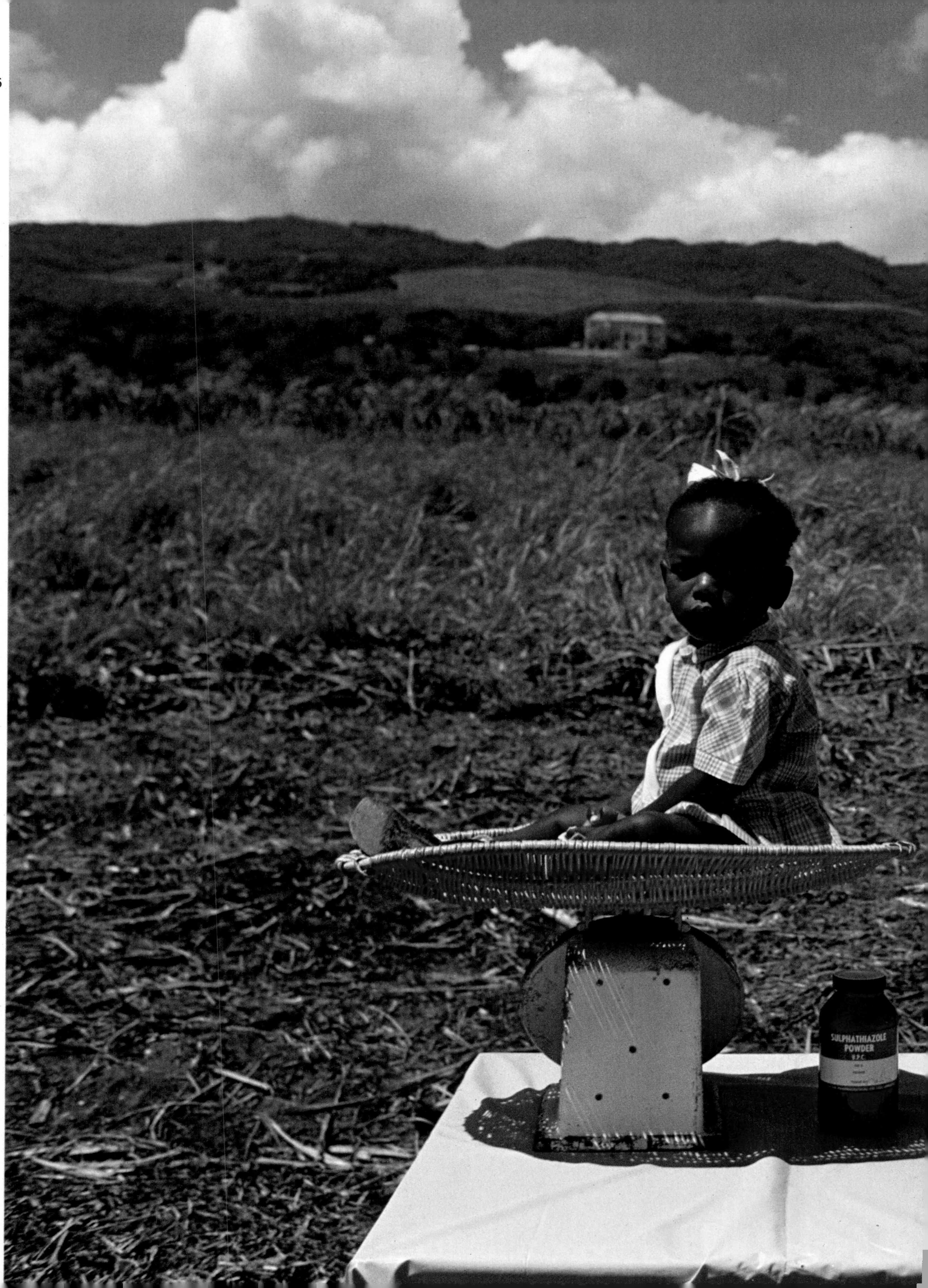
SULPHATHIAZOLE
POWDER
B.P.C.

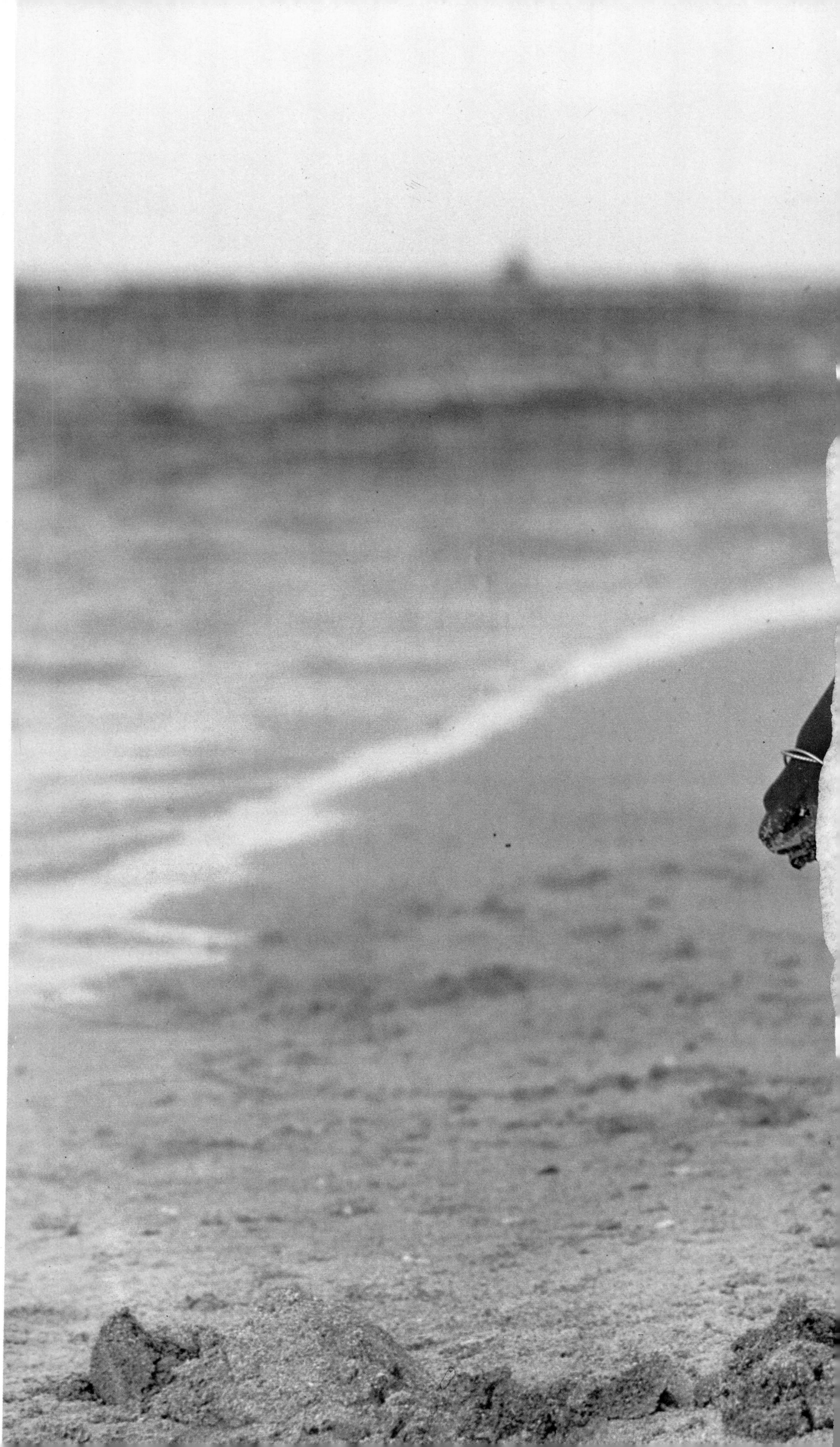

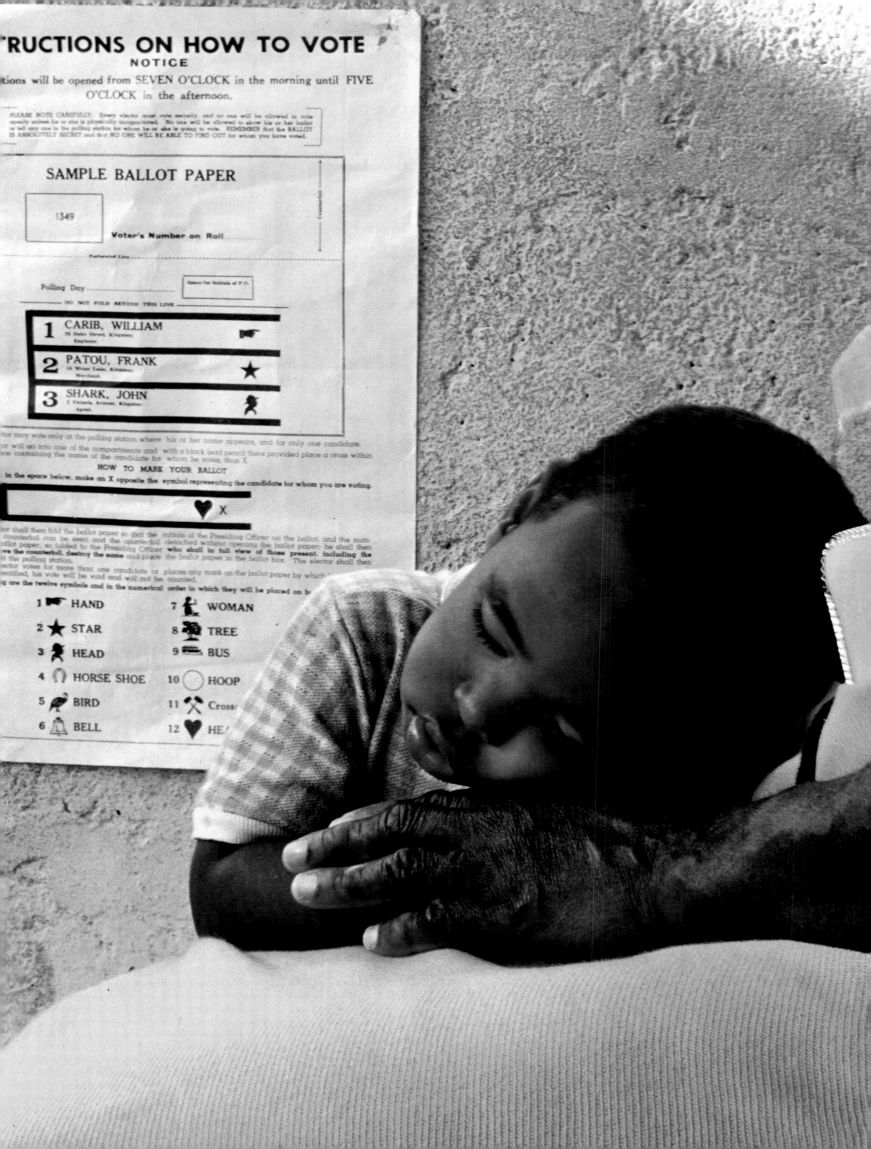

MILO
NUGGET
LACTOGEN
CASH
Horlicks
GORDON'S
DISTILLED LONDON DRY GIN
White Label
VitaFul
ORANGE
RELIEVE
COLDS
LAGER BEER
NORWAY SARDINES

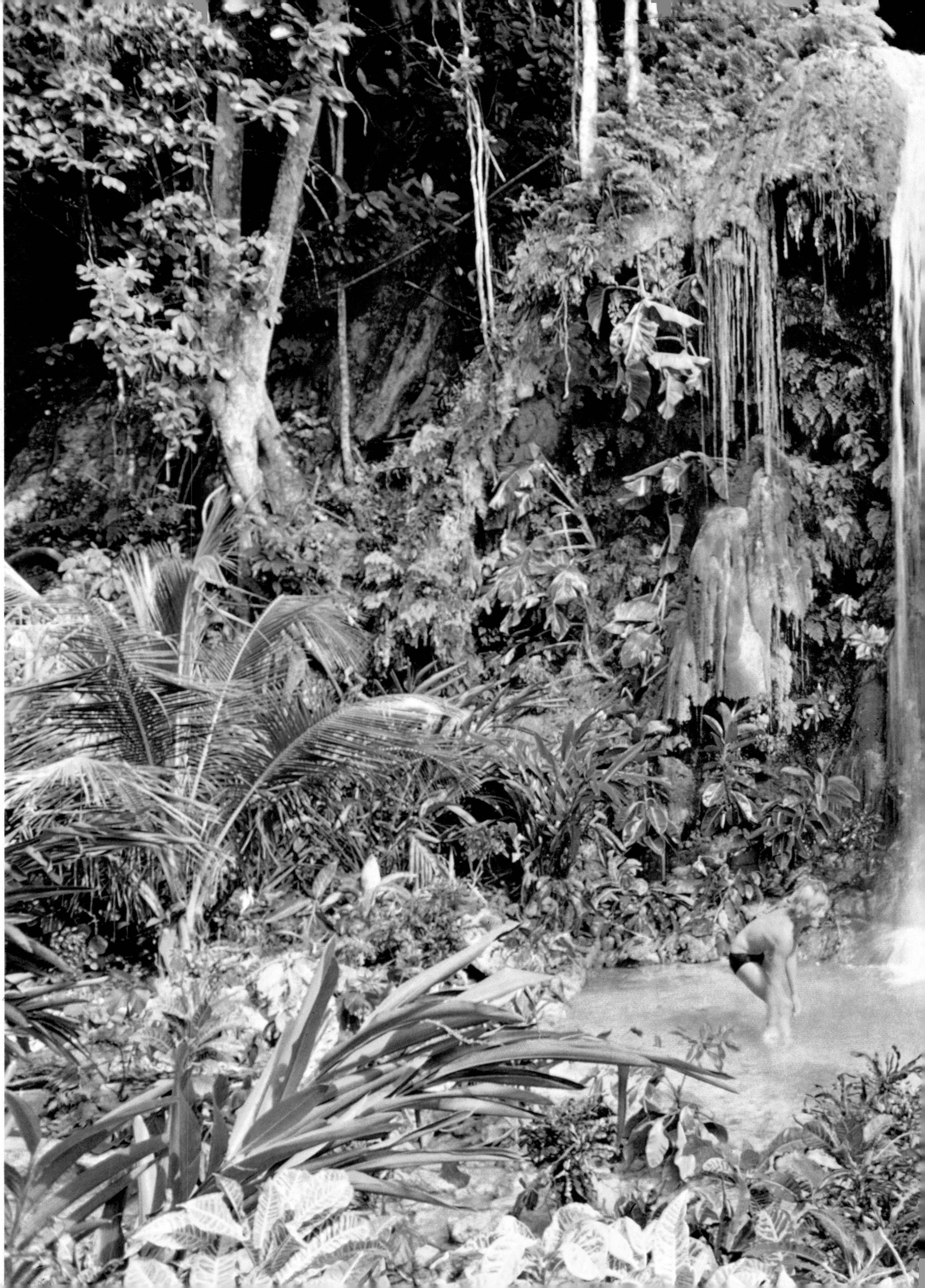

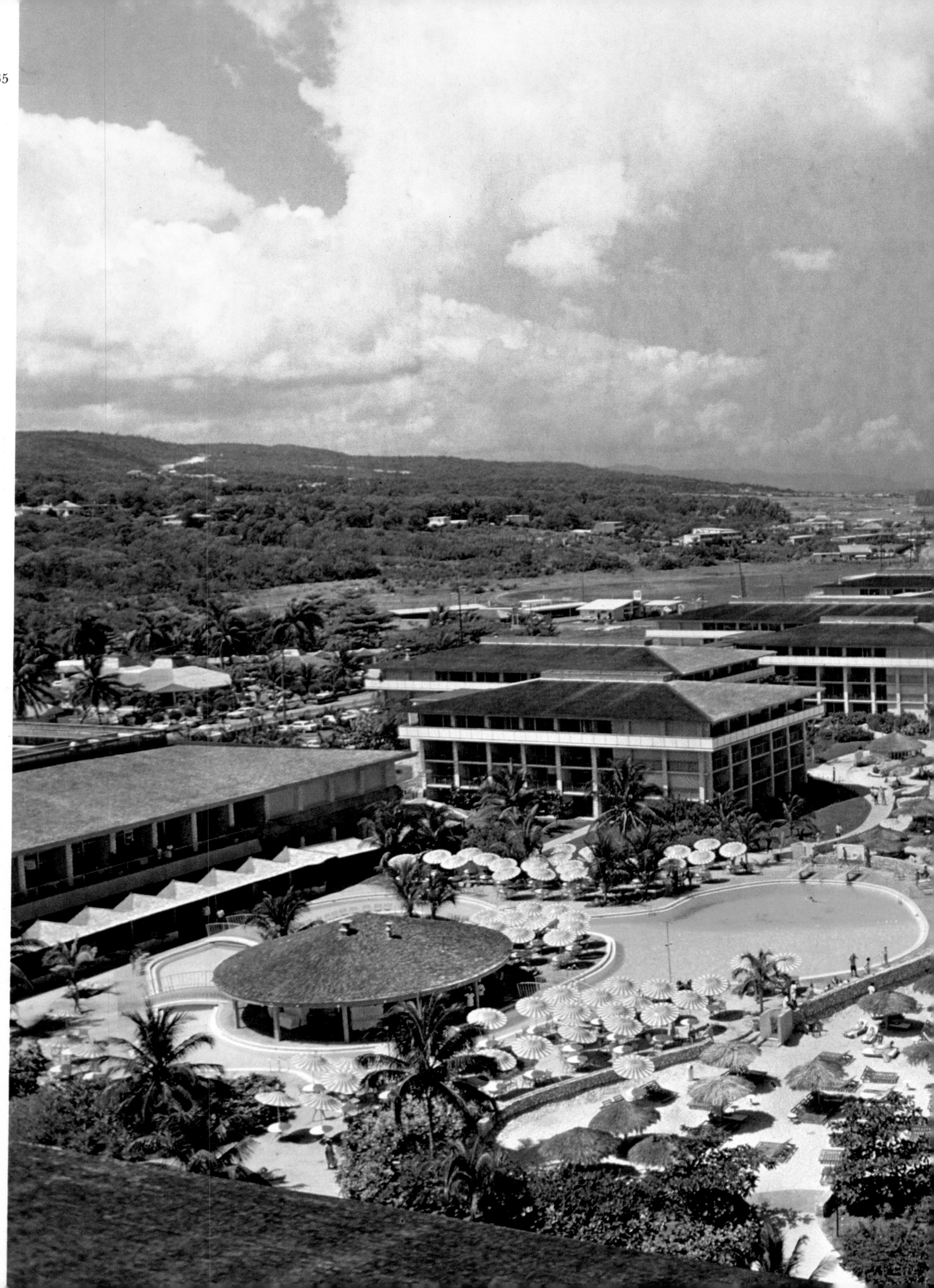

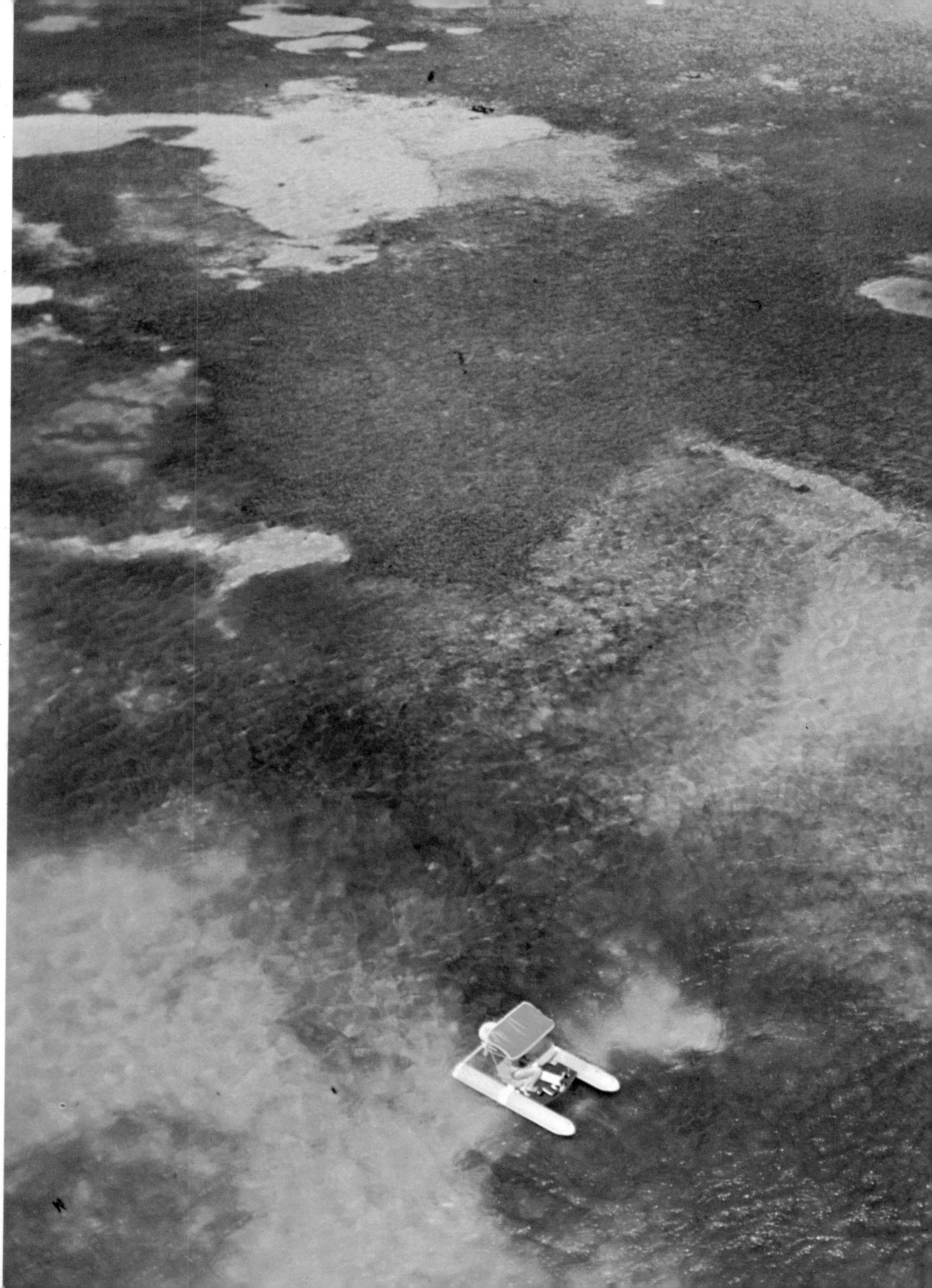

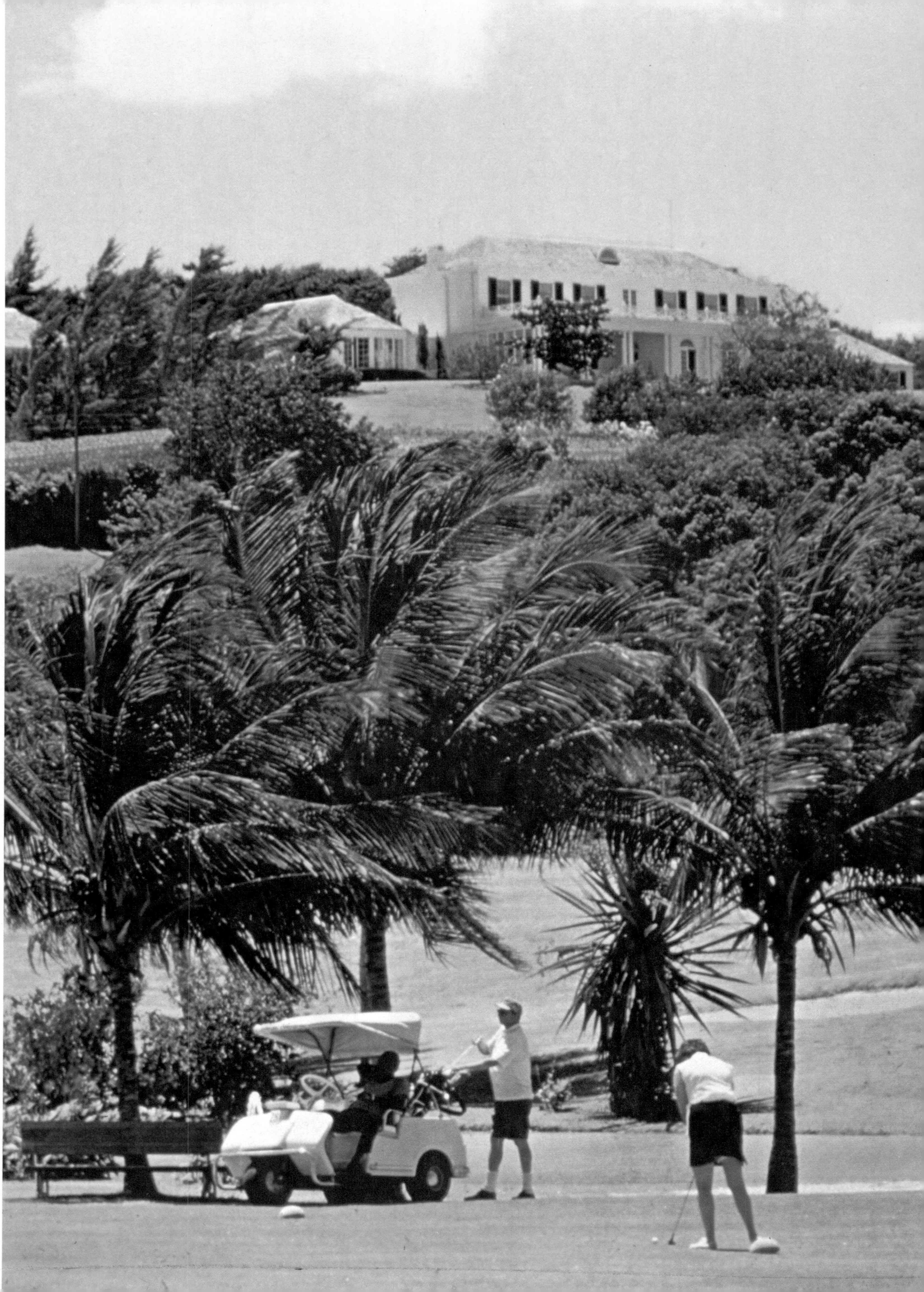

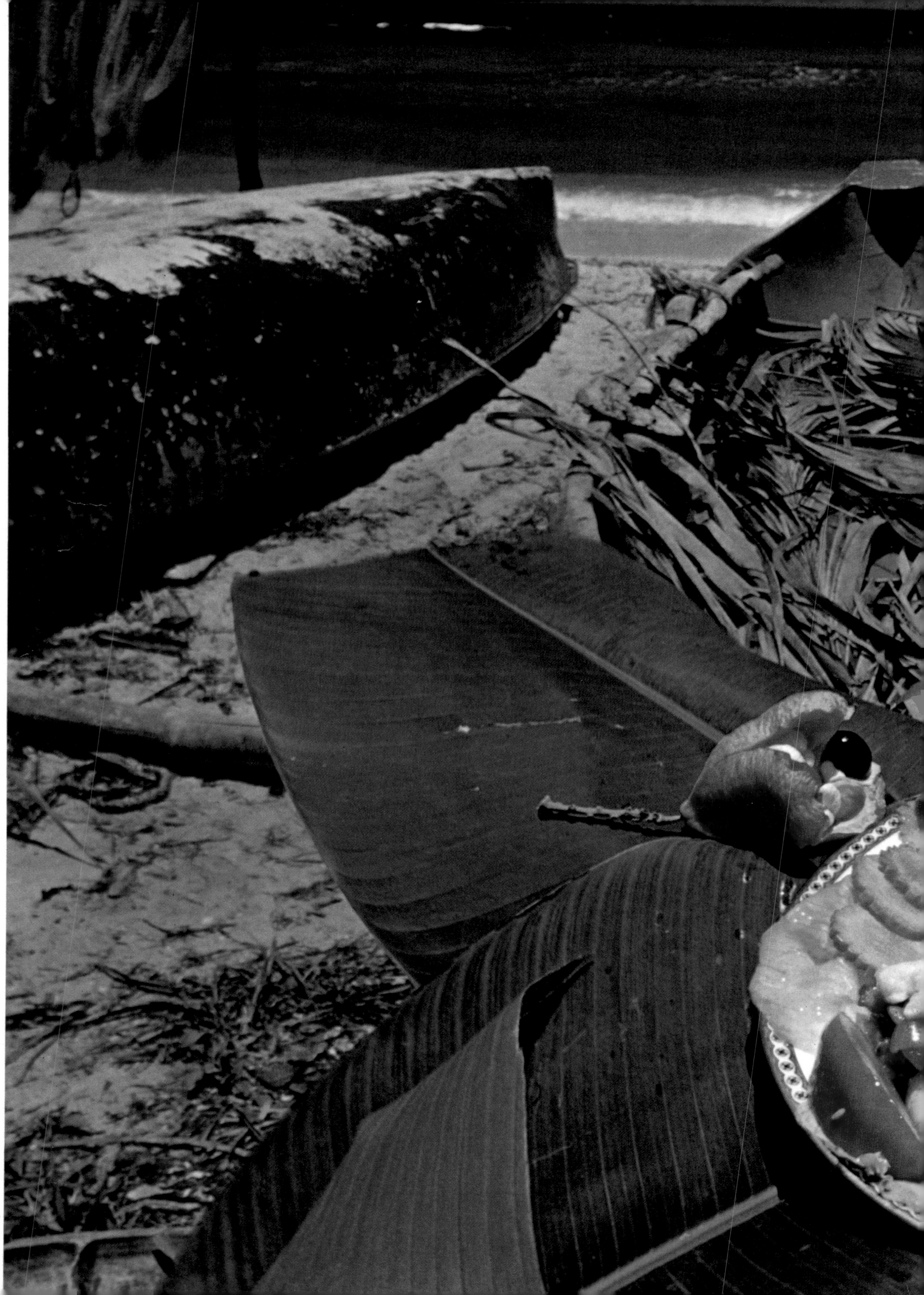

The Legend of Rose Hall

Annee Palmer of the legend was beautiful. She had a rich voice, black penetrating eyes, smooth black hair, small nose and mouth. Her complexion was lovely. She could be gentle, smiling—even childlike, according to legend.

But everyone was well-warned of the meaninglessness of this countenance. For Annee Palmer was also haughty, cruel, impatiently bored and easily provoked. She was in love with her own temperament, where it took her; from anger to deep sensuality. She enjoyed terror, tolerated no talk about her, or insurgence of any kind. Husbands and lovers who no longer pleased her met with untimely deaths. She was married three times.

John Palmer did not know what lay beneath the beauty of his bride of eighteen when he married her. When she wanted to please, Annee showed the greatest innocence, complained of helplessness and false accusations against her. Most deeds she claimed to be untrue and the product of gossip. Sometimes she admitted to having to use harshness, but only, she claimed, in self-defence or to establish discipline. At the same time, she could threaten anyone who took too lightly his possible doom at displeasing her with the very reputation she denied.

Annee had strength besides her cruelty. She had the power of a mind trained in sorcery. She believed in spirits and had the ability to project death fears on her slaves. She was the one plantation owner on the Island who was not excluded or intimidated by obeah. The slaves believed she spied on them and conjured up fiery apparitions which spelled doom to all who saw them.

At eighteen, Annee had just left Haiti. Her mother was English, her father an Irish merchant, who had come to Haiti attracted by the chance of making money under King Henry Christophe, who allowed white people to settle there.

As a little girl, Annee had become the favourite of a high voodoo priestess, who held considerable influence in King Christophe's court. Widowed and childless, she turned her attentions to Annee with trinkets and valuable gifts. Annee's parents encouraged the woman's interest because they felt her influence with the king could benefit them. It was this woman who taught Annee to believe in spirits, to regard the air as charged with the supernatural, over which she could gain control. She attended forbidden voodoo orgies, summoned by eerie drumbeats in the dead of night. She saw the fear the people had of the high priestess and was carefully schooled by the latter in the ways of creating this fear—black magic and death. The priestess convinced Annee that she had the powers of a god.

But the priestess died and Annee's parents died, leaving her very much alone in Haiti. It seemed a bad place for a single girl of her stature. She could have gone to England, but dreaded the conformity that would have been placed upon her. Thus she came to Jamaica.

John Palmer lived for seven years after their marriage. Annee claimed he drank, that the second husband went mad and the third married her for her money. The slaves said poison, stabbing and strangulation did them in one by one. Blood stains remained on the beautiful floor of at least one room in the Great House to attest to the murders, and that room was closed off.

In her solitary castle, Annee believed she kept even the spirits of the dead men in fear. For eleven years Annee Palmer ruled Rose Hall. After her husbands died, she ran the Plantation alone, with the assistance of an overseer and other white help. Since these men were usually outcasts or wanderers from English society, they cared little about the behaviour of the ruling or the slave classes. Whether she took them as lovers or not, Annee had contempt for them and regarded them as inferior. She indulged their habit of drink and cohabiting with the slaves as long as she could rely on them to get the Plantation work done and be as merciless as she was.

Despite her many lovers and the floggings that so excited her, she was always restless for some new exhilaration. One of her distractions (according to a chronicler of the period) was to get "into male attire in the evenings and, riding 'round the properties, lay her whip on the backs and on the bodies of any of the people whom she found out of doors and presumably doing wrong . . ."

She welcomed every opportunity for a dramatic display of anger. One maid who tried to poison her was

XV

convicted of the crime and executed in Montego Bay. Annee asked for her head and the request was granted. She then ordered an older slave and obeah master to carry the bloody head in a basket ten miles from Montego Bay to Rose Hall. At the Plantation, Annee had the head hoisted on a long bamboo stake, to fester and decay in the tropical sun as a warning to others who might have similar ideas of getting rid of her.

Although few people could have seen her go into the trance-like states when she was projecting harm on her victims or conjuring up the "Rolling Calf" or "Three-Legged Horse" (the apparitions of doom) in the night sky, there were slaves and white people who swore they had witnessed the apparitions and the trances. Doctors said they could do nothing for a slave who believed that he was under her death spell. Unless an obeah chieftain was successful in his rites to exorcise the evil spirit, the victims died. Sometimes there were slaves she feared. Sometimes they were slave women, who provoked a jealous rage over a man. It was rumoured that an apparition had been seen by everyone on the Plantation on the night of John Palmer's death.

"I wonder," says one of the men in H. G. deLisser's novel, *The White Witch of Rose Hall,* "if she is quite sane?" Another answers: "Pride, and the life she has led, and the power she has had over the slaves, may have unhinged her brain. That is quite possible. Inordinate vanity and fierce passions, in surroundings like these, may have unbalanced her, or insanity may be her heritage."

Despite the speculations, the white staff at Rose Hill did not really consider Annee Palmer mad; they saw in her actions extremes of behaviour that were practised elsewhere in the West Indies. The slaves did not concern themselves with matters of sanity, only with the fact that she was certainly a demon. Because she entered their realm of magical power, they were spellbound, but also intent on killing her.

She was finally murdered in her bedroom in the Great House in 1831 and buried on the Plantation in the east garden, where her grave can still be seen, "though it is now overgrown and surrounded by trees."

Rose Hall was left in the echo of its past, but with hopes for peace and rest after unrest. The beginning of a new democracy was dawning for the Jamaican people.

Up to the second decade of the 19th Century, the name and the Plantation held no particular mystery. But by then we are into the Jamaica of the mid-nineteenth century when many changes were taking place. The price of sugarcane had dropped and the Island was in financial trouble. Rebellion was everywhere, and looming on the horizon was the inevitable last hour for those who wanted to maintain the old rule. It was against this background of decay and transition that Rose Hall became the most extraordinary symbol of the time. ❀

Rose Hall and the Community

When John Rollins embarked on the challenging job of restoring Rose Hall, he, his wife and associates in Rose Hall Developments Ltd. committed themselves to the principle of corporate citizenship, working with and through the people of the immediate environment. It was *Jamaican* craftsmen and supervisors who collaborated in the exciting task of restoration.

The commitment lives on in the involvement of the Rose Hall planners in the development of the communities surrounding the restored monument and old estate.

The restorers first went to the heart of the matter—religion. Jamaicans are a deeply religious people. Their Emancipation from slavery was effected with the help of Christian missionaries, and the residue of their African heritage manifested itself in religious rituals which were the prime vehicle for their protests, sorrows and hopes during their three centuries of slavery. The first church built for the people of the Rose Hall area was the Mount Zion Church.

Zion—the fortress—was the sanctuary of God; and the Rev. Hope Waddell, a Scotch minister, selected its site on a hill commanding a spectacular view of the Caribbean. Hope Waddell had drawn his converts from the surrounding estates and on a Sunday morning would hold divine services where it was most convenient. He held such services in the then deserted mansion of Rose Hall. But by 1837 he was able to lay the first stone of the Church.

Mount Zion Church can still be described as he termed it, ". . . a conspicuous object . . . a crowning diadem of beauty."

Built with the willing hands of the former slaves... because by 1838, Emancipation had been declared... the Church took form from yellow bricks and red bricks brought as ballast in the holds of English sailing ships.

Former slave owners contributed material and loaned carts and cattle to haul the supplies up the steep hill. The building ". . . 66 feet long and 48 feet wide, with a gallery, and the whole cost, from the purchase of the ground to the hanging of the bell, including a session house, was fifteen hundred pounds sterling..." and was finished the last week of June 1838.

The Church served the neighbouring communities faithfully for many decades. The building withstood earthquakes and hurricanes, but finally succumbed when a mighty army of termites made a concentrated and determined assault on the roof structure and other wooden portions of the building. The termites were assisted greatly in their campaign by a faulty gutter bed system and several leaks which caused water to run freely into the interior. Eventually the timber became water-soaked and it was soon discovered that the building was unsafe for public use. So the building was closed in April 1966 and the congregation met in the Mount Zion Schoolhouse.

Within two years the Church was restored with the help of "friends of the Mount Zion district." The pastor and his congregation understandably see this act as a historic phenomenon. In recalling the story that the bell of Mount Zion Church rang all day and night on Emancipation Day, August 1, 1838, someone has asserted that Mount Zion's bell "still rings out the message of freedom, a freedom (this time) from mental slavery, ignorance, insensitivity and inertia."

Today, the Church serves the districts of Mount Zion, Chew Stick, Tryall, Rose Hall, Cornwall, Spot Valley, Kings Gate, Rose Hill, Lilliput, Long Bay, Flower Hill, Barrett Town, Palmyra, Dover and Little Ease — districts which all carry the quaint place-names in which the map of Jamaica abounds.

Education is no longer the job of the Church in Jamaica—at least not exclusively so. Government now plays a leading role because education is central to the strategy of development of the Island's people. Mount Zion School is the scene of many creative activities among the young — and all supported by the Rose Hall Development scheme. An annual art exhibition, continuing classes in painting for children between the ages of 6 and 15 and the encouragement of handicraft all point to an enlightened view on human development and growth. In 1969, Neville Budhai was employed by Rose Hall to instruct the students in various avenues of art. On Sundays, the red-robed choir of adults and children raise their voices in unison at divine services and the choir has become part of a Montego Bay Community Choir which travels to other parts of the Island to bring music to people in less fortunate circumstances. A basic school to catch the child at the vulnerable early years is a target of support as well; and, an educational fund has been established to ensure continuity.

Much else is planned for the eventual enrichment of the people and their community. But it is the concentration on the development of the young which gives to the community-mindedness of the Rose Hall Development scheme the meaning which it has. The arts contest among some several young Jamaicans produced work of high quality in the area of child-art and an essay competition on the Rose Hall Great House Restoration attracted some fifty eight contestants.

The involvement of the Jamaican people in the overall plans is an unusual thing in the style of management of many such projects by investors from abroad. The example set by the Rose Hall developers may very well help to bring out more corporate-citizen attitudes among investors who come into the Island.

It is in this way that true fusion of native Jamaican talent and foreign assistance can produce a climate conducive to healthy social and economic growth. It is a climate which is vital to the realisation of the dream of a new society, a new world-order rooted in justice, tolerance and love.

❧

Rose Hall Restored

The legend of Rose Hall will linger on. But with it now comes a new reality.

On Friday, February 26, 1971, the Great House was rededicated by the head of the elected government of Jamaica in the presence of a gathering of Jamaicans from all walks of life. Immediately following the ceremonies, guests from Jamaica and all parts of the world were given an inaugural tour of the newly-restored Great House.

Rising three stories high at the front, it is approached by a double flight of steps to the right and left which lead to the main floor through a central arched door. This Italian-inspired staircase approach (so dear to the hearts of those early Georgian designers, including Lord Burlington and William Kent of England) gives the desired feeling of ceremonial approach to a great country house. Lord Burlington himself used such frontal staircases in his villa at "Chiswick," which set architectural fashion for half a century in England. It is thought, however, that this terraced staircase was a later addition to Rose Hall and that the original entrance was of much simpler character.

There are three points about the design of the house which give an idea of its richness and complexity: first, the sweeping change of levels from the lower floor up the double staircase through intervening landings to the main floor; second, the entrance to the main hall or Ballroom through a mahogany arched doorway beyond to the southern end

of the building. The arched doorway of the entrance is flanked by rounded Tuscan columns, bearing the entablature which is mentioned in builders' guides of the period and edited by Abraham Swan and Isaac Ware.

The House thrusts forward some ten feet from its main body, having a width great enough to allow the placement of two great windows on either side of the entrance. This forward projection adds special interest to what might otherwise have been an overly austere facade. Corners of this projection as well as the angles of the receding elevations to the rear of this facade have the characteristic quoined rustication so often seen in Georgian Palladian Houses.

One is struck with the appropriately-placed windows, so often found in English houses of this time — a ratio of open space to solid area arrived at through close observation of Palladian and subsequent Georgian ideals.

Finally, there is the use of sumptuous and tasteful materials on the walls, in the draperies and in the appointment of the furniture. Georgian mouldings and their woodwork, rich mahogany, tall niches flanking the archway, giving controlled balance to the first elevation meeting the visitor's eye. A flood of lights from great windows (controlled by interior casements) gives a luminous vivacity suitable to this spacious room where lavish entertainment can be held. Great chandeliers provide evening illumination for the

magnificently proportioned Ballroom.

On passing through the great front entrance, the visitor will be struck by the contrast between the restraint of the exterior and the magnificence of the interior. ✿

The Great Staircase Hall— Lower Level

The Morning Room

The great staircase hall, which may be entered either directly from the south terrace or through the archway from the Ballroom, announces the mood of dignity and harmonious restraint characteristic of the 18th-Century Georgian houses. Pilasters similar to those in the Ballroom flank the two principal entrances.

A printed fabric of tropical birds and bamboo stalks on sunny yellow cotton decorates the walls of the hall. There is a touch of the Orient in this hand-screened print which is appropriately called "Chinese Bamboo." The Gallery has a rather relaxed ambiance in contrast to the other elegant and quite formal rooms on the main floor.

Two crystal chandeliers of French design are hung on centre at either end of the hall. On the east elevation to the right of the doorway into the dining room is an English-made mahogany gaming table which dates to 1760.

To the left on the north wall is an English mahogany Queen Anne-style dropleaf table flanked by two early 18th-Century William and Mary side chairs upholstered in sea-green velvet, and above them an early 19th-Century English family portrait.

Beside the door leading to the Morning Room is a tall case grandfather clock which was found at Cinnamon Hill, the Jamaican residence of the Barretts of Wimpole Street. 🌺

The seventeen hundreds ushered in the luxuries of the East—its rich silks, its china or porcelain, its delicate art which found its way into the homes of wealthy West Indian planters and their ladies via the holds of East Indian trading ships. And this reflection of the Orient is brought out particularly in the decor of the Morning or Breakfast Room.

The walls are covered in a turquoise and blue printed "Chinoiserie Toile" which is a reproduction of an 18th-Century Chinoiserie floral design and sets the oriental motif which is further borne out by the willow pattern design of the china setting on the central mahogany Hepplewhite two-part dining table. Queen Anne dining chairs of the same period are placed about the dining table. A pair of 18th-Century pewter candlesticks with glass hurricane shades adorn the table. While suspended above the table is a Dutch brass chandelier typical of those during the early years of the 18th Century. To the foot of the table nearest the door is a George II copper kettle resting on its warming stand.

To the left of the doorway leading into the study is an English oakwood Queen Anne serving table dating to about 1720. Above this table is a painting by the Dutch artist, Joost de Mompers (1565-1635).

To the right of the doorway is an antique English oakwood pewter cupboard (circa 1780) displayed with China Trade dishes and pewter.

In the southwest corner is an English oakwood William and Mary chest of drawers (circa 1700). While just inside the door leading from the lower gallery in the corner on the left is an early 18th-Century oakwood William and Mary side table. Resting on it is a continental copper and brass lavabo of the early 19th Century and on the wall directly above the lavabo is a tole or water container. Beside the lowboy is an oakwood brass-bound English bucket (circa 1800). 🌺

The Dining Room

The Ballroom

The Dining Room of Rose Hall has had its magnificent proportions enhanced by a beautiful Chinese wall covering made of rice paper. On it are depicted some 63 species of oriental birds.

The four-pedestalled Sheraton banquet table of mahogany banded with satinwood and ebony dominates the room and it is surrounded by a fine set of George III mahogany ribbandback dining chairs of Chippendale-style. A towering George III mahogany breakfront cabinet (circa 1780) dominates the west wall and contains a fine set of fifty pieces of 18th-Century China Trade porcelain having fish-scale borders and central rose motifs.

On either side of the windows on the east wall are two mahogany George III serving tables of the early 19th Century. Between the two windows on the north and south walls are a pair of George III inlaid rosewood console tables attributed to Thomas Hope (circa 1810). On the console table along the south walls is a covered venison serving platter, hallmarked, English Sheffield (circa 1820).

On the rear walls is a Sheraton-style buffet inlaid with ebony, satinwood and holly (circa 1800). Placed on this buffet are a pair of satinwood inlay Sheraton urns (circa 1800) designed for use as knife-boxes.

Over the centre of the dining table hangs an Adam-style chandelier of French Armolu and crystal. On the table, there is a George III Sheffield plate (circa 1800) epergne flanked by a pair of triple armed Sheffield candelabras, each bearing hurricane glasses (circa 1800). Other items on the table include two Irish Waterford glass decanters with silver coasters and two Spode dishes.

In the northwest corner of the room is a rare George III mahogany dropleaf, two-tiered, dumbwaiter (circa 1800).

The curtain treatments of the dining room are based on English Georgian designs, festooned and fringed for classic windows of this type.

A large stylized artichoke dominates the design of the draperies in this room. This motif, taken from an old Renaissance damask was designed by Franco Scalamandre for the dining room because he felt that the ancient symbol of hospitality is representative of the sumptuous dinner parties held here in years past. The celadon green silk yarn was custom-dyed to complement the colours of the oriental wallpaper. All of the tassels and trim are handmade and dyed to match the silk.

Two Chippendale armchairs are covered in a hand-woven silk brocade called "Floralia." Small golden pomegranates are scattered throughout the floral motif—and these too are an ancient symbol of hospitality. The dining chairs are upholstered in a diamond-shaped cut velvet in a shade of green which blends with silk damask. 🌸

On entering the Ballroom from the front terrace, one is immediately confronted with Georgian elegance and the atmosphere of restrained opulence of the Great House.

All is in symmetry and balance reflecting the careful observance of 18th-Century architectural precepts. Georgian mouldings similar to those found in such builders' guides as Isaac Ware's *Complete Body of Architecture* and Langley's *Builders' Directory* are seen in cornice trims and panelled dadoes, of mahogany

Two classical niches flank the archway opposite the entrance. Between dado and cornice the walls have been stretched with sixteen panels of magnificent brocade reproduced from the famous "Palm Tree" panels designed by Philippe de la Salle and woven originally for Marie Antoinette's salon during the reign of Louis XVI. The exotic scene of birds, butterflies and palm trees is most appropriate for this superb plantation house. The panels were woven in Italy on Jaquard looms and 68,000 cards were required to weave the design. After the panels were finished, Mr. Scalamandre hand-painted the outlines around the birds, butterflies and foliage in shades of golds, oranges and tans. The gold and green heavy silk used to cover the Ballroom chairs matches the colours in the wall-covering panels. Window seats are upholstered in matching plain background of the walls. The trimming and chair ties are of heavy silk, made by hand. All of these fabrics were especially woven for Rose Hall. 🌸

The Library

The Gallery— Upper Level

The Library, a square room entered from the right end of the Ballroom has a second doorway leading to the Morning Room. The walls are stretched in a beige, coral and gold damask having a flower and foliated design typical of mid-Georgian taste. Other characteristic textiles of warm brown and varying tones of coral are used on upholstered pieces in the rooms.

Opposite the Morning Room entrance facing north and between the windows is a George III fret carved English mahogany gaming table Chippendale-style (circa 1760) beside an English mahogany Queen Anne easy chair (circa 1760) which is upholstered in varying shades of brown and beige to create the famous Hungarian flamestitch pattern.

To the right of the window is a George III English mahogany inlaid slantfront gentleman's desk and a George III Regency mahogany caned chair with leather-covered steps (circa 1810) which can be folded back to reach the book shelves. Above the desk is an 18th-Century John Elliott looking glass (circa 1765).

On either side of the door leading to the Morning Room, are built-in mahogany book shelves holding leather-bound volumes and pieces of 18th-Century China Trade. To the left of the doorway there is a rare English mahogany Regency Canterbury (circa 1810) for holding newspapers.

On the west end of this side of the room is an English mahogany Queen Ann-style dropleaf side-table with a George III Chippendale easy chair (circa 1790) near it. Above the table hangs a "Portrait of a Lady" (circa 1750) attributed to Sir Peter Lely.

A brass chandelier of early 18th-Century character hangs from the centre of the library ceiling and is complemented by a pair of brass wall sconces of similar feeling at either end of the right window wall.

Beneath the chandelier are a Georgian tea caddy and a Delft platter on a rare English Georgian mahogany table (Chippendale-style) with exceptional carved shaft, legs and feet. And, on either side of the centre table is a pair of 18th-Century Charles II oakwood side chairs attributed to Daniel Marot. ✿

The main staircase leads to a spacious hallway off which the six rooms upstairs open. On the north wall there are two George III side-tables ebony inlaid (circa 1810) and in the centre stands a Jamaica George III mahogany pedestal table (Plantation history) with a china bowl mounted in Gold Dore' (French circa 1810) on it.

Between the door to the Crewel Room and the south wall is a mahogany corner cupboard, satinwood inlaid, English 18th-Century, Hepplewhite-style (circa 1780) and at the opposite end of the expansive hallway on the south wall is a tall case clock English mahogany inlaid, Hepplewhite-style Plantation history (circa 1780). The etchings of Jamaica Governors are of historical importance and the remaining ones in this set are in Annee Palmer's sitting room and in the gentleman's bedroom. ✿

The Crewel Room

The Toile Room

The use of India crewel was very popular in England and the islands. It was brought in by the East India companies that sailed to India and the Orient for import/export trade. The crewel design is hand-embroidered in wool on a coarse cotton ground. This one is the famous "Tree of Life" pattern with multi-coloured flowers and serpentine branches repeated throughout the cloth. Although this is a modern fabric woven by natives of the province of Kashmir, it is identical to the originals made hundreds of years ago. The fashion for quilted crewel, as used on the window seat, was an added luxury. A solid blue linen emphasizes the shade of blue wool in the crewel coverlet.

Blue linen edged in red silk trimming hangs from the four-poster bed of the late English Regency character (circa 1810). A small English Hepplewhite mahogany stand with inlay (circa 1780) is placed beside the bed and at its foot is an English oakwood chest, late 17th Century, Plantation history, which has a George III Chippendale mahogany bench (circa 1760) near it. Opposite the bed between the windows, an English walnut Queen Anne chest of drawers (circa 1720) is flanked by a pair of English George III Queen Anne-style mahogany and walnut chairs with stretchers (circa 1740). On the east wall opposite the door is an English mahogany washstand (circa 1810) with an ironstone pitcher, pewter wash basin and pewter bedpan.

An 18th-Century beechwood single-door armoire, of French Provincial origin with oakleaf and acorn carving, stands next to the door. ✿

A charming, cool green and white toile print is used throughout this bedroom not only on the bedspread and tester but on the walls. It was not unusual to use the same fabric simply because it was not only fashionable but more expedient to order just one design in large quantities when the trading ships brought goods from England and the Continent. This green and white toile de peu print is of nostalgic countryside scenes and is called "La Course Anglaise." The very old toiles were hand-blocked on cotton and this modern version is authentic in every detail including the hand-screening and country greens on ecru cotton ground.

The furniture is chiefly of mid-Georgian and later Georgian character. An English mahogany washstand (circa 1810) with a 19th-Century English engraving above it after C. Lorrain (Morning: published by J. Boydell, London, after James Peake), is placed against the wall balanced by an early 19th-Century French armoire of Louis XV-style with steel fittings, similar to many used in many other plantation houses in many parts of the Caribbean. A mahogany corner chair (circa 1800) with open fretwork vase-shaped splat is used at the George III English mahogany escritoire (circa 1800) which is placed between the two windows on the north wall of the room.

A china basin and pitcher are placed to the right of the doorway on an early Georgian washstand.

The four-poster bed of mahogany

Annee Palmer's Bedroom

is early 19th-Century type having heavy bedposts turned and carved in the late English Regency style. On the east wall is an English mahogany chest of drawers Hepplewhite-style (circa 1790) with an English mahogany looking glass and stand, shield shape, flanked by a pair of brass candlesticks (circa 1810). ❧

The use of red and the elaborate rose motif is indicative of the dramatic and passionate temperament of the legendary mistress of Rose Hall. The draperies and bed hangings are heavy white silk with a rose border hand-woven in a rich red. The tassel fringe on the canopy was hand-made in matching silk colours. Walls are covered in a Regency striped white silk. A "potty-chair" is upholstered in red and white cotton damask with tiny roses woven into the design.

In keeping with the elegance of the last proprietress of Rose Hall, it was decided to create a brocade having a rose motif and expressing the sentimentality characteristic of early 19th-Century decoration. This rose-bordered motif has been used for bed hangings on the great Jamaica bed so typical of plantation house furnishings in Annee's days and for the window draperies. To the left of the entrance stands a George II, Queen Anne-style English chest inlaid with satinwood, rosewood, cherry, walnut and mahogany (circa 1700). A papier maché perfume set rests on the chest. A late 18th-Century English mahogany tea table with carved pesdestal stands between two late 17-Century William and Mary walnut chairs of exceptional quality attributed to Daniel Marot. Above the tea table are hung two small oval portraits of the late 18th-Century English School.

In the northeast corner of the room to the left of the bed is placed a Georgian English mahogany cor-

ner cabinet with holly and ebony inlay (circa 1780). In the opposite corner stands an early Georgian basin and stand, having a tripod base and insoled paw feet (circa 1780). It is fitted with its original Rockingham bowl. In front of the north wall stands a 19th-Century English late Regency mahogany Thomas Hope daybed having heavily carved feet fashioned as dolphin heads and oliated arm rests and the shell motif at each end of the bed.

To the right of the entrance door is a Jamaican mahogany armoire in the French style (circa 1800). On the wall to the right of the bed is an English mahogany table Hepplewhite-style (circa 1800). An English George III mahogany bench is placed in front of the dressing table.

To the right of the door leading to the sitting room is an English Queen Anne George III walnut slant front desk, string and star inlay (circa 1720) with a chair of the same origin. ❧

Annee Palmer's Sitting Room

Gentleman's Bedroom

The room adjacent to Annee's bedroom is arranged as a boudoir/sitting room. The red and white scheme of the bedroom is continued here in variations of darker and lighter tones. Window draperies are in red self-toned flowered damask and have triple-festooned valances edged in red and beige tasseled fringe. An English mahogany slant-front desk and bookcase with glass doors (circa 1780) and a chair of the same period are placed against the west wall adjacent to the next bedroom.

Beside the desk is an English mahogany Chippendale easy chair (circa 1760). To the right of the door leading to Annee's bedroom is an English cane and satinwood lady's chair with painted decoration of the 19th Century (circa 1820) beside a round Georgian mahogany two-tier table having an English Rockingham 19th-Century tea service on it. Between the windows hangs a Chippendale 18th-Century mirror and directly below is an English or Scottish three-place mahogany settee (circa 1790) upholstered in deep red. To the left of the door to Annee's room is an English mahogany Queen Anne-style chair (circa 1780) next to a Georgian Pembrook dropleaf satinwood table on which rests a tea caddy painted in gilt on black lacquer.

A Chinese Coramandel lacquered armoire of the Queen Anne period having short cabriole legs stands near the door to the gentleman's bedroom.

The deep red silk damask draperies feature romantic love birds, bow-knots and garlands of roses. Two wing chairs and the desk chairs are upholstered in a satin and moire stripe of red, cream and ribbon weave of blue-grey. ❦

This room, according to the complex legend of Rose Hall, is said to have been the bedroom of one or more of Annee's successive husbands and after the mysterious death of the last occupant, it was closed off permanently.

A virile colour-scheme of soft rust, gun-metal grey and brown establishes the masculine character of this bedroom with heavily carved four-poster bed of late English Regency character from which is hung a large scale brocade topped with a scallopped and tasseled tester repeated in these colours. On the left side of the bed is placed an English mahogany desk (circa 1760) Jamaica history, with a George III side chair. Against the window wall to the right of the bed is a French Provincial oak armoire of Louis XV period.

In the northwest corner is a small late Georgian washstand with China Trade wash basin, goblet and other appurtenances. Opposite the bed between the windows stands an English walnut William and Mary chest inlaid with satinwood (circa 1720). An English walnut Queen Anne armchair (circa 1730) is beside it in the corner to the right. Behind the chair is an English George III mahogany tilt-top tea table.

On the left wall of the entrance to Annee Palmer's sitting room is an English walnut Queen Anne dressing table (circa 1720) with an English mahogany and Chippendale gesso looking glass (circa 1780) above it. The wall sconces are 19th-Century French gilt bronze. ❦

Guest Room

This is the most elegant of the three guest rooms on the second floor of the Rose Hall Great House. It immediately reflects Annee Palmer's favourite rose motif which is hand-woven in cotton on silk and linen. Here again, the same fabric is used in the entire room. The custom of putting fabric on the walls was very popular in that era as it served as an insulator against the heat as well as a very decorative upholstered wall covering. The cotton loop fringe used to trim the bed hangings is made to pick up each of the colours in the floral brocade.

The great bedroom is also provided with an elaborately-carved four-poster of late Regency design. At the bottom of the bed is placed a Georgian English brass and mahogany blanket chest. To the left of the bed is an English Mahogany George III corner basin-stand (circa 1790), with a 19th-Century Staffordshire bowl, pitcher, and covered soap dish. To the right of the bed is a single late 18th-Century French armoire and a 19th-Century plantation clothes-tree beside it. In front of the armoire is an English mahogany side chair (circa 1780). Adjacent to the door is a small commode (circa 1820). Opposite the bed between the windows is an early Georgian, English mahogany, tilt-top, tripod base tea table (circa 1760) flanked by rush-bottom English Regency chairs of early 19th Century.

An English walnut Queen Anne chest of drawers stands on the west wall (circa 1730) to complete the room. The colour scheme of this room is based on the rose pattern brocade linen, having various tones of rose and green against a natural linen background. ❧

Index of Illustrations

20.
Religion has always played an important part in the lives of young and old Jamaicans and on Sunday morning scores of people from the Rose Hall area will walk many miles up the mountain to the Mt. Zion church to hear the pastor's sermon and the children's choir.

21.
The Mount Zion School and the Infant School are supported in part by the owners of Rose Hall. Here, Mrs. Cameron, a teacher at the Infant School, marches with her youngsters in a Jamaican flag parade.

22.
Playing together today and working together tomorrow; little steps in the sand now, but a big step into the future at Rose Hall.

23.
The future of Jamaica belongs to the young and old and becomes the interest of all at election time.

24.
Rose Hall Social Life: The after church social when members of the Mt. Zion congregation enjoy homemade ice cream (left) or a young couple's wedding reception (right) at a Rose Hall seaside restaurant.

25.
Rose Hall Workers: The development of Rose Hall depends on many Jamaicans from the Plantation overseer (left) to the basket weaver who sells her hats and bags in the Great House Shoppe.

26.
Rose Hall Artists: Neville Budhai (left) exhibits his own work and teaches art to the Mt. Zion children once a week. Kingston born cabinetmaker, Thaddeus Kirkland (right) moved to Rose Hall to help on the restoration of the Great House.

27.
The Rose Hall Chinese Grocery, a surplus of Jamaica's finest.

28.
The Rose Hall Dungeon creates its own "Witch's Brew," as prepared by Great House bartender, Mr. Lester Bell (right) or the exotic tall "Rum Cooler" (left) with a sugarcane swizzle.

29.
Rose Hall Specialties: Young Jamaican wood-carvers (left) are very talented and will custom carve your own head statue in one day. In the hills of the Plantation, Jamaican women collect the fresh fruits and flowers via donkey (right).

30.
Following inherited British tradition, the Mount Zion Cricket Team puts on their whites every Saturday noon to meet with teams from other local districts.

31.
Rose Hall Educators: Mrs. George Robertson (right), President of the Mt. Zion school board, in front of her Chew Stick home and Pastor Earl Thames, a Rhodes scholar who dedicates his time and talent to the church and school.

32.
Two typical Jamaican beauties enjoy the grand pleasures of Rose Hall and the surrounding community.

33.
Rose Hall is a tropical paradise filled with the unexpected. Here, near Cinnamon Hill, a waterfall fed by mountain-cooled streams and surrounded by lush natural beauty attracts its own beauties.

34.
Vacationers enjoy a romantic picnic beneath a flame tree on Cinnamon Hill (left) while residents (right) practice polo on the lawn of the Cinnamon Hill Great House, the ancestral home of Elizabeth Barrett Browning.

35.
The Caribbean-modern design of the Rose Hall Holiday Inn forms a geometric pattern on the white beach between the green Jamaican hills and the blue Caribbean Sea, with an outline of Montego Bay resting on the distant horizon.

36.
The Rose Hall Holiday Inn beach rests beside a calm cove filled with crystal clear water where rafts and sailfish can float undisturbed, while skin divers explore the coral reefs.

37.
A contemporary great house in Rose Hall's Spring Farm overlooks a round of golf at the Rose Hall-Half Moon Country Club.

38.
Watching Rose Hall water sports instructors master the waves of the Caribbean is a sport within itself. Here, a life guard goes surfing on a sailfish.

39.
Ackee and Saltfish, as much a part of Jamaican life as sand and surf, as seen on the white beach at Success Pen.

40.
Mango Hummingbird, the largest of the three kinds to be found in the island, and common in thickets and woodlands around Rose Hall.

41.
The Great House kitchen becomes a background for the tantalizing tastes of Jamaica, an abundance of fresh island produce interpreted in a poetic still life portrait.

42.
A vibrant explosion ignited by Mother Nature, a single Hibiscus bloom bursts to life in one of the many gardens of Rose Hall.

43.
Annee Palmer lives on today in legend only, but the famous Palms planted for each of her brutally killed lovers still thrive on the peaceful beach of Rose Hall.

XXIX

Acknowledgements

Text by
Rex Nettleford—(*editor*)
T.A.L. Concannon
John W. Rollins
Linda Ashland
Olive Senior

Photographs
Slim Aarons
Arnold Newman

Design and Layout by
Frank Zachary (*Director*)
Norman S. Hotz

Printed and bound by McGraw-Hill Far Eastern Publishers (S) Ltd. — Singapore

Contributions

West Indies Reference Library,
Kingston, Jamaica, W.I.
National Trust Commission,
Jamaica, W.I.
The Tatler, London, England
L.M.J. Henry
Dorothy Charley
Stanley Winder, Barnett Estates
Agnes Grant
Marjorie Marsie Hazen
Casey Wondergem
Lisa Salmon
Rose Hall Developments Limited
Jamaica Tourist Board Photographs
Airwing of Jamaica Defence Force
and most of all to
The People of Jamaica.

28th June, in the
ing, Overseer on
nsolation can be
iends in North-
evinced by the
ded to pay the
rth.

lt. Miss Sarah

25th ult. Isaac
by all who had
with him.

nst. Mr. Geo.
onsolate wife
man's hospi-
ll classes of
be long felt
ny years.

y, Capt. T.
te, of Bris-

n the 30th
laughter of

n her pas-
es Brown

Nor are they
r friends, wh
rt the
is g
lizing of the
will keep to
four houses, and
ejected, when on
obtained possessi
What will the
" White wome
will, in general,
their slaves to be
will even stand by
and punished in th

As in the course
the Island, we nev
ragoes; and as we
has been present